# INTENSIVE GARDENING ROUND THE YEAR

# INTENSIVE GARDENING ROUND THE YEAR

**by**

**PAUL DOSCHER**

**TIMOTHY FISHER**

**KATHLEEN KOLB**

with drawings by Kathleen Kolb

THE STEPHEN GREENE PRESS  Brattleboro, Vermont

This book has been produced in the United States of America. It is designed by Irving Perkins Associates
and published by The Stephen Greene Press, Fessenden Road, Brattleboro, Vermont 05301.

*Library of Congress Cataloging in Publication Data*

DOSCHER, PAUL, 1950–
    Intensive gardening round the year.

    Includes index.
    1. Vegetable gardening.    2. Organic gardening.
I. Fisher, Timothy, joint author.    II. Kolb, Kathleen,
joint author.    III. Title.
SB324.3.D67  1981        635'.048        80–21921
ISBN  0-8289-0399-9 (pbk.)


PUBLISHED MARCH 1981
*Second printing November 1981*

# CONTENTS

# ACKNOWLEDGMENTS

WE WISH to thank the many people who helped us as we gathered material for this book. There were intensive gardeners in fourteen states who made themselves and their gardens available to us for questions and photographs. All of them were generous with their time, most of them spending a couple of hours patiently answering questions and showing us their gardens. Seldom did we give them much notice, but all of them were very accommodating. Especially kind were John and Betsy Hibbard, Louise and Drew Langsner, Carolyn and Earl Lawrence, Janney and David Munsell, Vic and Betsy Sussman, Adam and Bonnie Tomash, and Ray Wolf, who welcomed us not only into their gardens but into their homes, sharing meals or offering accommodations during our travels.

Dr. Frank Eggert was extremely patient with our questions and gave us his time both at his home and at the University of Maine. Eliot Coleman at the Coolidge Center for the Advancement of Agriculture put us on the trail of many of the gardeners with whom we have been in touch, and made his unusual library available to us, for which we are most grateful. Leandre and Gretchen Pois

son have had a large influence in what we have to say about solar intensive methods. Leona Collier at the Greensboro Free Library was sympathetic and helpful in obtaining for us the obscure books we needed quickly. Patti Nesbitt deserves special thanks for her enthusiasm and for helping us to locate a number of the gardeners we interviewed. Eleanor Adams was also helpful in contacting intensive gardeners, as were the Maine Organic Farmers and Gardeners Association, and the Boston Urban Gardeners.

Other gardeners whose help is very much appreciated, and whose intensive gardens appear in photographs through this book are: Bobbie Allshouse, Winnie Amato, Liz Blum, Tony Bok, George Crane, Barbara Eggert, David Emery, Galen Fisher, Irene Fuderer, Barbara Greenspun and Jane Schmelk, Joe Howko, Richard C. and Nancy Jo Harrison, K'uan Choi Heung and Shui-Ying Lam and the other gardeners at Unity Tower in Boston, Paul Ladd, Eric Laser, Kenneth and Marjorie Lauer, Norm and Sherrie Lee, Luis Lopez, Hilde Maingay at the New Alchemy Institute, Jim Markstein at Ramapo College, Dianne Mathews and Jeff Moyers at the Rodale experimental farms, Ray Nelson, Heather and Don Parker, Warren Pierce at Carmel in the Valley, Kathy Sheridan, Sam and Elisabeth Smith, Don Sunseri, Robin West of the Claymont Society, Charles Woodard at Goddard College, and Dr. Micheal Wirth at New England College.

Edna Knapczyk was helpful in lending books, and Laurette Perron graciously translated some nineteenth-century French material. Ralph and Sally Fisher have both assisted with proofreading.

Our special thanks are due to Bill Eastman, who has been a very patient editor, and Deborra Doscher, for her advice and encouragement.

# INTRODUCTION

INTENSIVE GARDENING is a system of growing plants to produce a maximum of crops from a limited amount of space. Intensive methods involve using very rich soil and careful planning to assure that space and materials are not wasted. Most often the intensive garden is one where plants are grown on raised beds in which every square foot of soil is constantly in use by a succession of healthy, intermixed, closely spaced, and productive crops. With the use of simple glass- or plastic-covered solar energy capturing devices this succession continues through most of the year, further increasing the productive capacity of the garden. Additionally, intensive gardening is successful in reducing some of the labor involved in weeding, watering, pest control, and other tedious tasks.

You may have already seen this type of garden. Intensive flower and herb gardens are common today. Here plants are spaced closely, and carefully planned to insure successive bloom while other plants are just getting started. The purpose in the flower bed is purely decorative, but the same techniques are used in the intensive vegetable garden to make optimum use of space. For many people the ability to grow a great many vegetables in a small area is their primary reason for gardening intensively (see Figures 1–6). They may have only a limited space available, or a small garden may be all they can comfortably handle. Surprisingly, however, the majority of people we have visited during the preparation of this book could have had bigger gardens, but use intensive methods because of the excellent results they were able to achieve.

Other people are attracted to intensive methods because they are a more efficient way to use water, soil amendments, energy, and labor. This is particularly true of gardeners who use only hand tools. Quite a few people feel that working in raised beds saves them a lot of uncomfortable bending and squatting as compared with "flat" gardening (see Figures 10–12). Others make raised beds to improve soil drainage in wet and soggy areas.

Many of the gardeners we interviewed have given an artistic dimension to their intensive gardens. Because of the dense spacing and the use of raised beds, there are many possibilities for creative expression both in the interplanting of each bed and in the overall arrangement of the beds within the garden.

**Figures 1–6** *The ability to grow a great many vegetables in a small, compact area is one reason for gardening intensively.*

**Figure 1** *Garden of Kenneth and Marjorie Lauer in Pennsylvania.*

**Figure 2** *Garden of Kenneth and Marjorie Lauer in Pennsylvania.*

**Figure 3** *Garden of Kenneth and Marjorie Lauer in Pennsylvania.*

**Figure 4** *Garden of Richard C. and Nancy Jo Harrison in Massachusetts.*

**Figure 5** *Garden of Richard C. and Nancy Jo Harrison in Massachusetts.*

**Figure 6** *Garden of Richard C. and Nancy Jo Harrison in Massachusetts.*

**Figure 7** *Excellent results are achieved with intensive methods in large gardens as well as small. Garden of Ray and Linda Nelson in Maine.*

Because of the quantity of plants growing in the small area of intensive beds, the beds lend themselves to being covered by glass or other materials to capture the sun's heat and shield the plants from colder outside air. This creates a modified microclimate in which the growing season can be extended to include every season, even in northern climates. A wide variety of devices exist for extending the growing season. To simplify references to them, we have chosen to refer to them as "solar intensive devices." Regardless of their differences they all use captured solar energy at the time of year when plants most need it. We will describe many of them and their applications in the chapters devoted to solar intensive gardening.

This book has been written for the gardener who has had some experience in conventional gardening and is familiar with the basic principles that produce successful crops. It will discuss the intricacies, the essentials, and the pros and cons of both intensive and solar intensive methods. We have tried to provide all the information necessary to the success of intensive methods, but have left to other books the task of listing specific cultural practices for individual plant species. We have also included the suggestions and practices of a number of intensive gardeners who have been generous enough to share their gardens and experiences with us.

We have attempted to give as broad-based in-

**Figure 8** *Intensive methods are used in herbaceous flower borders. Garden of David Emery in Maine.*

**Figure 9** *Garden of David Emery in Maine.*

**Figure 10** *Intensive beds can even be created on pavement. Garden of Diane Matthews in Pennsylvania.*

formation as possible, and the basic principles of intensive gardening we describe are valid in all climates. But we have had the majority of our personal gardening experience in northern New England, so it naturally follows that much of our emphasis is toward the concerns of a cold climate gardener.

Since we are organic gardeners, we favor building fertility through organic means. This means that we do not endorse the use of chemical fertilizers or soil amendments. Nevertheless, some people believe that one can supplement an organic soil with conservative use of chemical fertilizers without ill effects. Even so, an error in the application of these chemicals can be disastrous to the natural health of the soil.

The beauty of an organic soil, high in humus content, is that it is likely to suffer only minor chemical or nutrient imbalances. The natural soil process is capable of overcoming most problems if it is respected and supported by the gardener. Thus we believe that organic gardening is much more appropriate to the needs of the home gar-

dener, who generally lacks extensive knowledge of chemistry and soil science.

You will notice we do not include information on chemical pest control. The pest control measures we describe may seem minimal relative to those described in other books, but they are all we have found to be necessary to grow high-quality vegetables in the fortified soil of intensive beds.

**Figure 11** *A bathtub can become an intensive bed. The height of a raised bed is an asset to people who find bending over difficult. Garden at the Rodale New Farm in Pennsylvania.*

**Figure 12** *Boxed beds at the Rodale New Farm in Pennsylvania.*

Many people have taken up gardening to counter the rising cost of buying vegetables. Price increases occur, to a considerable extent, as the result of the massive amounts of energy required to produce crops with chemical fertilizers and pesticides, process them, and then ship them thousands of miles across the continent. This "long-distance" food further represents a loss of the more tender and flavorful varieties of vegetables once available in local markets. The more modern replacements, bred for their appearance and ability to withstand shipping, often lack the flavor and nutritional value of locally grown produce. So our food not only costs more, but it does less for us.

In the long run, more important than the high price or questionable quality of commercial vegetables or the amount of petroleum consumed in their production, processing, and transportation is the ongoing destruction of our nation's soils. Soil is essential to our continued survival, yet it is treated by much of modern agriculture as a consumable commodity. Topsoil, and the organic matter it represents, is being depleted, poisoned, and eroded away at the rate of millions of tons per year. This process not only threatens the stability of our agriculture, but results in water pollution and the disruption of many essential natural ecological systems.

It is not feasible for an individual tilling a thousand acres, using large machinery, to give the same care to the soil as the small family farmer or the home gardener who cultivates only a tiny area. Yet we must have intimate concern and care for the soil if our civilization is to survive. The need to provide a rich and dynamic soil for dense planting of crops makes the intensive gardener into a soil builder rather than consumer, a caretaker of a precious natural resource.

Although the vegetable garden produces much during the warm months, even the gardener who preserves, freezes, or root cellars enough food for

**Figure 13** *Garden at the Rodale Old Farm in Pennsylvania.*

xiv

the rest of the year either does without fresh green vegetables during the cold months or remains dependent upon imported produce. Solar intensive gardening offers an alternative. It is possible for the solar intensive grower to produce many of his or her vegetables on a nearly year-round basis. Fresh green crops from the garden in winter provide not only a financial saving but better nutrition than that available from frozen or "less than fresh" produce from the supermarket shelves. Although building the devices to produce these crops can require a substantial investment, it is one that can pay itself back many times over (see Figure 14).

Intensive gardeners trade the labors of weeding, tilling, and such for other labors. Building soil is no simple chore, and the intensive methods demand a lot of persistence and just plain hard work, particularly during the first few years. Also required is good planning and horticultural hygiene. A lazy or sloppy gardener is not likely to have a much better intensive garden than he is a conventional one. Haphazardness in the intensive garden can bring disaster at worst, disappointment at best.

We must also concede that a large quantity of organic matter must be added to the soil to build intensive beds. At present the organic gardener can still take advantage of the failure of modern farmers and society in general to fully use these organic "waste" materials. But as the prices of chemical fertilizers rise to the point where they cost more than the value of what they produce, and as society comes to recognize the value of the wide variety of material now considered "waste," these organic materials will no longer be so readily available. Fortunately, this is not an insoluble problem, for green manures, crop rotations, home and urban compost, and the use of human waste are all potentially plentiful substitutes for the manures gardeners use today.

Lastly, the fact that gardening is a very pleasant process is sufficient reason to grow your own vegetables rather than let someone else do it for you. Every gardener feels a sense of pride and satisfaction when harvesting his or her crops, and most find pleasure in the time they spend working in the garden. We have found that intensive methods both increase our pride in producing beautiful, flavorful crops and make the time we spend growing them more enjoyable and rewarding.

This is not to say that intensive gardening is the only good way to grow vegetables. There are many examples of nonintensive vegetable gardens that satisfy our concerns for building and maintaining a rich soil and produce high quality vegetables. Likewise, the solar intensive devices we use are not the only way to create protected microclimates to extend the growing season. Gardening is not an absolute art. Each gardener is different, each with his or her own set of circumstances, problems, and solutions. Understanding this, we offer this book with the knowledge that intensive gardening is a successful method for many people, and we hope it will introduce you to the same pleasures and productiveness that intensive gardening has provided us.

**Figure 14** *Solar devices make fresh green crops possible in the winter garden. Garden of Timothy and Kathleen Fisher in Vermont.*

PHOTO BY TIMOTHY FISHER.

## NOTE ON TERMINOLOGY

People call raised-bed gardening by a number of names, but the most frequently used is "French Intensive" gardening. This is somewhat of a misnomer, since the original French Intensive system that developed in Europe involved much more than just gardening in raised beds. It also included a focus on season extension by gardening under glass in order to capture the heat of the sun and fermenting manure. Furthermore, the French had no monopoly on the idea of gardening in solar and manure-heated enclosures, as the idea has been used for centuries.

It is not our intention to establish who should get credit for inventing either raised-bed methods, or the method of covering beds with climate-controlling devices. Instead we have simply chosen to call these methods by the names "Intensive" and "Solar Intensive," respectively. We feel that these terms accurately reflect what the methods are all about and allow us to include in this book a great variety of ideas regardless of their origin.

# 1

# A HISTORICAL PERSPECTIVE

Kathleen Kolb and Timothy Fisher

INTENSIVE GARDENING methods are as old as gardening itself, and their history can give us a perspective on our own efforts. The past offers us a deeper understanding of the present, and hence equips us better to deal with it. This is especially true, I think, in situations requiring "low" or "appropriate" technology. In these instances history often has the precedent and methods that, combined with modern materials, can offer workable solutions. Small-scale intensive gardening is a good example of this.

Although this history is limited mainly to Western traditions, being the primary antecedent of intensive gardening in America, it should be recognized that intensive cultivation has been practiced around the world for thousands of years.

The types of gardens people make are invariably determined by the value and availability of land and water, the tools and people available to do the work, and the climate. Other factors that shape gardens can be aesthetic, including current fashion and personal taste. Throughout history intensive-type gardens have been made in situations where land or water was dear, and where human labor using hand tools was the main available source of energy (see Figures 15 and 16). Where climates or seasons necessitated special care for plants to flourish or survive, intensive methods were easily broadened to include protective elements. In fact, the care and attention given to plants in an effort to modify their climate were generally practical only on an intensive level or scale.

Oriental cultures have a very old tradition of intensive gardening, developed in response to the need for their land to support a very high density of population. The general pattern in China was to grow culinary vegetables intensively and cultivate cereal crops extensively in the field. A sixth-century agricultural encyclopedia, the *Ch'i Min Yao Shu,* gives directions for protecting plants, including shading them in summer, wintering them under mulch in pits, and warding off frost in garden and orchard with smoldering fires. As one Chinese writer points out:

Lucid apprehension of the natural requirements of plants does not mean passive waiting. Quite the contrary, as the old Chinese saying . . . [human resolution can overcome Heaven's destiny] goes, the Chinese peasants have the unquenchable determination to wrestle with any crop under the most unfavorable

1

**Figure 15** *These raised beds near Nuwara Eliya in Sri Lanka are part of a longstanding tradition of intensive agriculture. In this overpopulated land where food crops compete for space with the cash tea crop, small family market gardens such as this one combine raised beds with irrigation and terracing to capitalize on land and water.*

PHOTO BY FRANK OATMAN.

conditions by their incessant labor. By observing and fulfilling the demands of the objects of cultivation, rarities can be produced in the most unpromising spot and time.[1]

In other situations, when land is extremely precious, gardens have been made on water. "Chinampas" are an example of floating gardens that evolved in pre-Columbian Mexico.

They originated in land famine. When the Aztecs first came from the north into the Valley of Mexico, they were made slaves by their more powerful and civilized neighbors; even later, when free, they were at first poor and weak, and confined to the marshy lakeshore which nobody else wanted. So they built on piles out into the lake, because what dry land they did have was too valuable for the raising of crops to be used for building. Hence their cities in the water, and their great causeways. But they also MADE land: They built rafts of reeds and rushes lashed together with tough roots, and onto them they piled soil dredged up from the shallow bottom of their lake, which, consisting largely of decayed vegetation, was very fertile. Raft was joined to raft,

and artificial, floating islands were formed as much as 200 feet long, and for the most part about four feet deep. The larger and older "Chinampas" had small trees planted on them, as well as plots of flowers and vegetables for market and even a hut for the gardener to live in. By using a long pole the gardener could punt his floating garden from shade to sun or sun to shade, or nearer to his market. At times it seems that scores of these floating gardens could be seen gliding about the surface of the lake.[2]

Floating gardens also exist on Dal Lake in Indian Kashmir. These are intensively cultivated patches of former swamp existing amidst the houseboat culture on the beautiful mountain lakes.

## EARLY EUROPEAN KITCHEN GARDENS

It seems that classical Western tradition was similar to that of the Chinese in including distinct cultures for field crops and garden vegetables. The essential elements of intensive gardening are spelled out in this description of a Roman kitchen garden.

[1] Shih Sheng Han. *A Preliminary Survey of the Book CH'I MIN YAO SHU: An Agricultural Encyclopedia of the 6th Century* (Peking: 1962), p. 36.

[2] Edward Hyams. *A History of Gardens and Gardening* (New York: Praeger Publishers, 1971), p. 124.

**Figure 16** *Indians in the Southwest cultivate their pepper plants intensively in sunken beds. From* The Story of Gardening *by Richardson Wright (New York: Dodd, Mead & Co., 1934).*

The productivity of these garden plots when under irrigation is astonishing: catch cropping and succession cropping are essential features, and with a sufficient supply of manure, every square yard of the garden is under cultivation; the seasons become virtually undistinguishable, and the return per manhour of effort is extremely high.[3]

The novelty of out-of-season fruits and vegetables was produced in Roman times with the heat of fermenting manure and the use of sheets of transparent minerals such as talc and mica. (Sheet glass was not known until the third century A.D.) Plants were sometimes grown in a basket of dung with a mineral slab for a cover. Pits were also used, warmed with manure or a masonry furnace, and likewise covered by a thin plate of talc or mica. This evolved into a primitive forcing house or *specularium,* in which heat was supplied by small fires around the walls, by heat ducts built into the walls, or by hot water.

Grapes, peaches, roses, and lilies were all forced in these structures. Once, when Emperor Tiberius was ill, his doctor prescribed that he eat cucumbers every day. These were grown throughout the winter in his *specularium.* Columella's *De Re Rustica,*

[3] K. D. White. *Roman Farming* (Ithaca, N.Y.: Cornell University Press, 1970), p. 49. Copyright © K. D. White 1970.

a classical Roman agricultural text, gave directions for less sophisticated forcing techniques, including ancient equivalents of pits, cold frames, and hotbeds.

There is no doubt that those Romans who enjoyed forcing houses and their fruits were members of the aristocracy and could afford such luxuries. This did not remain so forever, and though kitchen gardens continued to be intensively cultivated, methods of forwarding crops artificially seem to have languished with the wealthy class who had supported them. Although the style of the Roman kitchen garden provided the basis for vegetable gardening in medieval Europe, its refinements faded except in the monasteries, which became the guardians of horticultural traditions.

In Germany, Albertus Magnus, a Dominican philosopher and theologian, practiced the arts of forcing that the Romans had developed. Albertus was known as one of the greatest scholars of his time, as well as a fine horticulturist. One story describes how he received King William II of Holland at his monastery in 1249. It was the sixth of January, and in spite of the season Albertus was able to show King William flowering plants and fruit trees bearing ripe fruit he had forced in the cloister garden. This was so strange that people suspiciously called it witchcraft.

**Figure 17** *A garden of raised beds, 1470. From* A History of Gardens *by Edward Hyams (New York: Praeger, 1971).*

Medieval gardens were often laid out in beds with paths between them (see Figure 17). Culinary and "physic" herbs, fruits, and vegetables grew together in these gardens. Vegetables received less attention in this period than they had in Roman times, as meat had slowly become a more important element in the diet. Many plants, however, were cultivated for medicines and dyes.

Garden beds were raised for both practical and decorative reasons (see Figure 18). Some writers advised their use to improve soil drainage for plants particularly sensitive to wet ground. Garden benches were made by seeding a raised bed of the proper height with grass, often interspersed with small wildflowers (see Figure 19). The sides of these beds were made of brick, boards, or wooden lattice. Medieval illustrations show square and rectangular raised beds in pleasure gardens.

Kitchen gardens were usually surrounded by a wall, an important part of the garden (see Figure 20). Indeed, our word "garden" stems from the Middle English and German words for enclo-

**Figure 18** *Raised beds in a garden, 1542. From* A History of Gardens *by Edward Hyams (New York: Praeger, 1971).*

**Figure 19** *A garden bench and flowers grown in a raised bed, 1460. From* A History of Gardens *by Edward Hyams (New York: Praeger, 1971).*

sure—a wall was at one time implicit in the meaning of the word. In his *Encyclopedia of Gardening* J. C. Loudon writes of the abundant produce grown in market gardens near Vienna with this comment: "They are without walls, and, indeed, look more like fields than gardens."[4] Often fruit trees and vines were trained along a kitchen garden wall, and vegetable beds were bordered or mixed with flowers and herbs. This is still a European tradition. An example of such a garden was that of Sir Thomas More, whose garden at Chelsea overlooked the Thames. In it the fruit trees were trained along the walls, and the beds were laid out in regular rectangles.

The kitchen garden at the Ettlinger castle in Germany had twelve-foot-high stone walls surrounding and partitioning it. The walls were covered with wooden trellises, to which peach, apricot, and apple trees were trained. This was apparently characteristic of nearly all garden walls in Germany at the time Loudon was writing. This particular garden wall, however, had rafters projecting outward two feet just under the coping. These supported rolls of straw matting, which could be unfurled over the trees to protect the blossoms from spring frosts.

[4] J. C. Loudon. *An Encyclopedia of Gardening* (London: Longmans Green and Company, 1865), pp. 172–73.

Garden walls provided not only shelter from wind and storm and support for trees and vines, but gave a south-facing border, which has always been an important part of the garden. In old gardening manuals it is advised that early vegetables and salads be planted out in this sheltered, sunny spot (see Figure 21). Not only was the wall itself among the most elementary forms of plant protection, but it offered support for more sophisticated means, such as the mats described above and glazed sash. In some instances walls were heated by means of flues conducted through the masonry. This, coupled with the use of glass against the wall, constituted a primitive forcing house. Whether or not garden planners were aware of it, an added advantage of these masonry walls was their thermal mass, or their ability to absorb and store heat from the sun, radiating this heat back out as the surrounding air cooled, thus helping to moderate temperatures.

**Figure 20** *A garden with raised beds around the wall, 1490. From* A History of Gardens *by Edward Hyams (New York: Praeger, 1971).*

**Figure 21** *A walled garden as shown in* The French Gardiner *by John Evelyn in 1672. From* The Story of Gardening *by Richardson Wright (New York: Dodd, Mead & Co., 1934).*

## KINGS' FEASTS AND ROYAL GARDENERS

Gardens were made not only for private use, but also to produce vegetables for sale. Much labor, glass, and manure were spent in intensively cultivated gardens to provide the courts of Europe with fresh vegetables and fruits out of season. These were often shipped surprising distances.

Loudon reports that before 1500 many common vegetables were exported to England from Holland, supposedly because the English did not properly understand how to grow them (see Figure 22). In his *History of England* David Hume wrote that "It was not till the end of the reign of Henry VIII [mid-1500's] that any salads, carrots, turnips, or other edible roots were produced in England. The little of these vegetables that was used was formerly imported from Holland or Flanders. Queen Catherine, when she wanted a salad, was obliged to dispatch a messenger thither on purpose."[5] In speaking of the 1600's, Alicia Amherst explains that "there had for long been a fair supply of vegetables in England; but when anything early, or out of season, was wanted on great festive occasions, it was procured from abroad, chiefly from Holland."[6] The Dutch must have had considerable skill as growers to acquire this reputation, and they had a distinct forcing system, using pits (presumably with sash lights) and low houses by the early 1700's.

At this point in history forced produce was still the extravagant luxury it was in Roman times, and its history is one of kings' feasts and royal gardeners. It was not just the English nobility who relied upon Holland for early fruits and vegetables, but all the courts of Europe, including France, until the reign of Louis XIV.

In time court gardeners in all the countries of northern Europe produced vegetables out of season, though the extent to which they did so was limited by the wealth of the country. Thus Loudon, in chronicling the horticulture of Denmark in the early 1800's, gives the Danes much credit for

[5] David Hume. *The History of England,* as quoted in Loudon's *Encyclopedia,* pp. 283–84.

[6] Alicia Amherst. *A History of Gardening in England* (London: 1896), p. 259.

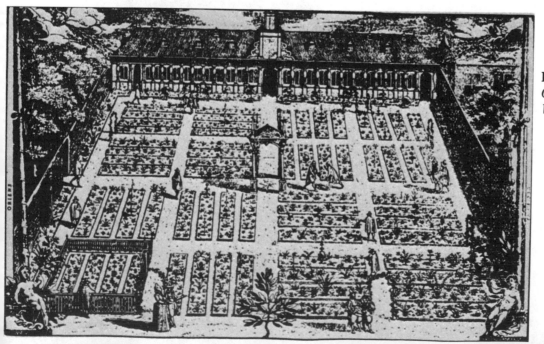

**Figure 22** *The Botanical Garden at Leiden, by J. C. Woudamus (Holland, 1610)*

their forced produce, especially considering the climate. In Sweden, on the other hand, although the gardeners were considered successful, he describes the season as short: ". . . and there is not yet sufficient wealth to admit of much forcing, or of forming artificial climates to any extent."[7]

Using glass to grow early vegetables is mentioned in Olivier de Serres's encyclopedic work on French agriculture, published in 1600. Louis XIII's gardener, Claude Mollet, was said to be a great pioneer in forwarding produce using manure hotbeds covered with glass sash.

## SIMPLE FORCING METHODS

This is about the same period that glass bell jars began to be used for covering one or more plants, giving them a warmer environment. Bell jars have been recorded in horticultural use in France since 1623. The term used for them there was *cloche,* which literally means bell (see Figure 23). These same glass bells have a long history of use in the laboratory, where they were used to contain a gas or vacuum, or to display a specimen. "Whether it was chance or some experiment that first brought the cloche from the alchemist's bench into the garden is a matter for conjecture. The fact remains that the bell glass became very popular in France at an early date and ultimately formed the basis for a great industry."[8] (see Figure 24.) Alchemy required the use of many plants and plant extracts, and it is entirely possible that a gardening alchemist first inverted the hollow glasses over growing plants, creating a minigreenhouse.

The use of these jars is mentioned in English books by John Parkinson, a London apothecary, in 1629. His book, *Paradisi in Sole Paradisus Terrestris,* describes using them over growing melon plants. He also suggests growing the melons on a slightly sloping hotbed, protecting them with straw when necessary.

Many simple ways to protect plants were used and recommended in the books of this time. Straw mattresses were supported over growing beds in

[7] Loudon, *An Encyclopedia of Gardening,* pp. 177 and 189.
[8] Louis N. Flawn. *Gardening with Cloches* (London: John Gifford Ltd., 1957), p. 14.

**Figure 23** *A bell jar cloche.*

the same way that autumn finds sheets, blankets, and plastic draped over gardens in our own time. To supply early blooms as well as edibles, plants were brought indoors in anything from a pot to a large box on wheels which could be rolled in and out. Manure was used in hotbeds and around plant protectors to give added insulation as well as radiant warmth. Cloth and paper were used to ward off frost in the same capacity that more expensive glass was.

In the seventeenth century a number of tender plants were coming to England from the New World. One of these was tobacco, which was started on a hotbed, then transferred to a south-

**Figure 24** *An enclosed garden from* The French Gardiner *by John Evelyn, 1672. Note the bell jars on raised beds.*

facing border sheltered from the weather. A variation on the stove-heated masonry wall was a wall made of boards, the heat supplied by a hotbed of dung piled up against the back. Fruits were trained on this wooden screen, the front of which was covered with glass. This technique was apparently in common use long before more sophisticated glass forcing and hothouses appeared in England.

## KITCHEN GARDENS IN PURITAN NEW ENGLAND

New England's gardens in the seventeenth century were basically an English import, like its people. For reference they had, at least initially, the same books relied upon in Europe. Their gardens were separate from orchard and fields, and each household was largely self-sufficient. By necessity the garden was expected to support a large number of plants for food, medicine, and dyes, creating a very diverse garden. Everything the Puritans planted was useful, in keeping with their belief that God had made the earth and everything on it for man's use. These gardens were usually made of raised beds to insure proper drainage, and because the limited area of the beds made it feasible to control and improve the soil quality.

Early New England gardens were enclosed with a wall or fence. This was essential as protection from wandering domestic and wild animals; it was also representative of the European tradition of the gardener. Along the inside of the wall a wide, raised border surrounded the garden. The other beds varied from simple oblong shapes to intricate geometrical patterns, depending on the affluence and artistry of the gardener. They were narrow enough that the gardener would never need to step in them while tending the plants. Paths were quite wide to prevent plants along the edges from being damaged. This was more of a concern then than in contemporary kitchen gardens, since the colonial garden was a place for visiting as well as for growing plants. It was the custom for people to walk and talk together in the garden (see Figure 25).

The beds were filled with a mixture of manure (or fish, which the Indians had taught them to use) and good earth. They were edged with boards, stones, or even sheep shank bones, and the good soil from the surface of the paths was scraped off and put in the beds. The paths were covered with gravel or something else that would drain well. Placing the garden on a slight slope was advised for severe drainage problems.

Perennial plants were grouped together, as were the annuals, which needed to be resown each year. Intercropping was used to save space and trouble.

**Figure 25** *A garden of sixteenth-century England with raised beds and wide paths.*

In *Paradisi* Parkinson suggests edging beds of squash or melons with cabbages and mixing onion, radish, and lettuce seeds to broadcast in a bed where they would all come up together, even though they would mature at different times.

## THE DEVELOPMENT OF FORCING AND MARKET GARDENING IN EUROPE

In France, at this time, an expert grower named Jean de La Quintinye was the director of the King's Fruit and Kitchen Garden for Louis XIV at Versailles. His book, *Traité des Jardins Fruitiers et Potagers,* published in Amsterdam in 1690, was said to be the best work on growing fruit and vegetables in his generation. It was translated into English in 1693 by John Evelyn, a famous English horticultural writer, under the title *The Compleat Gard'ner.* Apparently La Quintinye was quite a genius, and especially successful at producing early and out-of-season vegetables and fruits, which he forced on more or less scientific lines. Through his skill the king enjoyed asparagus in December, lettuce, radishes, and mushrooms in January, cauliflower in March, strawberries in April, peas in May, and melons and figs in June. La Quintinye must have been highly valued, for he received a yearly bonus equal to twice his annual salary. Though he is sometimes credited with developing a forcing culture into a system, the elements of such a system had, as we have seen, already been in use for quite some time in one place or another.

One source states that Huguenot refugees, arriving in England in the 1680's, brought a French gardening system with them, which they practiced in their gardens around London. However it may have evolved, the beginning of the 1700's in England was a marked contrast to the centuries before, when many vegetables had been brought from Holland. The English diet was gradually changing to include more vegetables, and market gardeners around London were not only growing a greater variety of them, but beginning to stretch their season, learning to force produce for sale. Philip Miller, a distinguished English horticulturist, noted these developments in the preface to the 1765 edition of his *Gardener's Kalendar.*

The improvements which have been made in the art of Gardening, within fifty years past, are very great; so that we may without presumption affirm, that every part of this art is in great perfection at this time in England, as in any part of Europe. Our markets being better supplied with all sorts of esculent plants, through the whole year, than those of any other country; and these in their several seasons are afforded at so cheap rates, that they are become a great part of the food of the poor: to which we may in part attribute the abatement of those violent scorbutick disorders, which formerly raged so much in this country.[9]

Two things seem to stand as major landmarks in the development of forcing skill in England. One was Samuel Collins's 1717 treatise on growing melons and cucumbers, including protecting them with frames and glass. The other was the presentation of two cucumbers to King George I on New Year's Day, 1721, by a nurseryman named Fowler. It was not long before artichokes, asparagus, cucumbers, and melons were being raised on hotbeds for market. By 1748, when the Swedish horticulturist, Peter Kalm, traveled through England on his way to North America, intensive market gardening had become quite impressive. The growing beds were raised and sloped slightly to the south.

... most of them were at this time (February) covered with glass frames, which could be taken off at will. Russian matting over these, and straw over that four inches thick. These contained cauliflowers some four inches high. In the rest of the field were "bellglasses," under which also cauliflower plants were set 3 or 4 under each bell-glass. Besides the afore-named beds, there were here long asparagus beds. Their height above the ground was two feet; on the top they were similarly covered with glass, matting, and straw, which had just been all taken off at midday. The asparagus under these was one inch high and considerably thick.[10]

The elements of intensive forcing culture up to this time—hotbeds, glass lights, bell jars, and hand

[9] Philip Miller. *The Gardener's Kalendar* (London, 1765), p. vi.
[10] *Kalm's Visit to England,* translated by Joseph Lucas (London: 1892), as quoted in Amherst's *History of Gardening,* p. 260.

glasses,[11] and the straw mats and mulches used for insulation—were similar in other intensive market gardening systems in Europe, though examples like Dutch light gardening and French gardening were distinct in their particulars. In Holland growing in forcing pits and frames with glass lights had for long been quite successful, and into the 1800's the skill of the gardeners was such that melons, grapes, and pineapples were sent to the London and Paris markets and sold for prices lower than the English growers could compete with.

## THE SPECIALIZATION OF INTENSIVE MARKET GARDENING IN FRANCE

In France an intensive market gardening system had also been developing, with gardens springing up in the environs of Paris, close to both the markets and the source of manure on which the system so depended.

> Before the French Revolution these *maraîchers* [market gardeners] were all affiliated to a guild, and important questions relative to their trade were constantly discussed. . . . Very little is known as to their trade during the French Revolution except through the authors of fiction, who frequently introduce the horse and cart of a market gardener to further the escape of their heroine. In 1820, however, these market gardeners began the forcing of Cos lettuce under cloches which were altered in diameter and height to suit the methods employed. The composition of the glass was also experimented upon until the favourable greenish tint was obtained.[12]

The French were said to excel in the production of winter lettuce on hotbeds covered with glass. This lettuce was in great demand in the Paris market. Loudon points out that vegetables played a more important role in the French cuisine than in the English, and that enormous quantities were purchased by institutions such as hospitals as well as by the general public. He reported that the vegetables were extremely fine and large due to the quantity of manure used and the benefit of daily waterings. Though the market gardens in the environs of Paris were generally small and cultivated intensively by hand labor, he noticed a few that were cultivated by plough and had more in common with field culture. By the middle of the nineteenth century it was estimated that there were over 1,000 *maraîchers* in the Paris area, their gardens averaging 1⅓ acres each.

The Paris gardeners had the benefit of fine seedsmen, and varieties of vegetables were developed specifically for their trade. Not only did these family companies deal in seeds, but also in information about the culture of vegetables. Out of their experience they published comprehensive texts on growing the plants they sold seeds for.

In the early twentieth century the number of market gardeners in operation around Paris had increased by only one or two hundred, but their holdings had, on the average, nearly doubled in area to 2½ to 3 acres. The French system by this time had developed into a very specialized method, which is, to a large extent, what made it profitable. This had been encouraged by keen competition between the Paris growers and was no doubt aided by the work of seed companies and guilds or unions.

Maximum efficiency was achieved by well-planned intensive cropping procedures, improvements in materials, and the use of modular appliances for which standardized designs had evolved through time. The lights, panels consisting usually of 16 glass panes and similar to window sash, were 4 feet 3 or 4 inches by 4 feet 5 inches (see Figures 26 and 27). Their relatively small size made them fairly easy to handle. Also, the narrow width of the area under glass made it possible for the plants to get the moisture they needed by capillary attraction from the pathways when the weather was too severe to remove the lights for watering. Wooden frames were used to hold the lights high enough off the ground for vegetables to grow under the

---

[11] Hand glasses are described in Loudon's *An Encyclopedia of Gardening*, p. 548, and were made in different styles. They were composed of many small panes of glass set in a lead, copper, or iron framework, and were portable. Their function was the same as that of bell jars.

[12] P. Aquatias. *Intensive Culture of Vegetables on the French System* (London: L. Upcott Gill, 1913; and Harrisville, New Hampshire: Solar Survival Press, 1978), pp. 5, 6.

**Figure 26** *Carrots and cauliflowers growing under lights in a French garden in the early twentieth century. From* The French Garden *by C. D. McKay (London: Associated Newspapers, 1908).*

glass. The frames were from 6 to 9 inches and shorter along one side so that the lights would slope gently toward the south. This gave a good exposure to the sun as well as a little shelter from the north and made the surface of the glass drain properly. The frames were 4 feet 5 inches by 13 feet, carried three lights each, and were placed end to end in rows running as close to east/west as possible.

Cloches were still an important gardening appliance. The best ones came from Lorraine and were 15 inches high and 17 inches in diameter at the base. Each held close to 6 gallons of water, weighed 5½ pounds, and was made of clear glass

tinted slightly blue to offer protection from strong sun (see Figure 28). At one time they had been made with a knob on top, but this had acted like a lens, focusing the sunlight and burning the plants growing under the cloche. Consequently newer cloches were made without knobs. The cloches were arranged to fit onto the same size beds that were made for the frames. Straw mats were used in the evening and in poor weather to cover both cloches and lights (see Figures 29 and 30). These were longer lasting than loose straw mulches and easier to deal with, as they could be rolled up.

To prop open the frames and cloches for ventilation special "tilts" were made with several

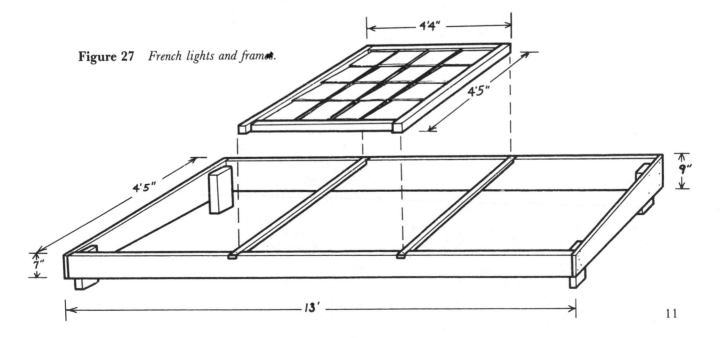

**Figure 27** *French lights and frames.*

4'4"
4'5"
9"
4'5"
7"
13'

**Figure 28**  *Bell jar cloches over lettuce in a French garden in the early twentieth century. From* The French Garden *by C. D. McKay (London: Associated Newspapers, 1908).*

**Figure 29**  *Rye straw mats were used to cover the frames and lights at night or in bad weather. From* The French Garden *by C. D. McKay (London: Associated Newspapers, 1908).*

**Figure 30**  *Frames, lights, and mat coverings. From* The French Garden *by C. D. McKay (London: Associated Newspapers, 1908).*

**Figure 31**  *Lights ventilated so as to avoid drafts*
*From* Garden Farming *by Lee Cleveland Corbett*
(*Boston: Ginn & Co., 1913*).

notches. The different notches of these props allowed varying amounts of air to get to the plants. Care was taken always to ventilate the appliances so that they would not be open facing the wind (see Figure 31). This was both to protect the plants and to keep the wind from catching under the glass and perhaps lifting and breaking it. The notches in the cloche tilts were made at such an angle that the lip of the cloche resting on the notch would slide off and close itself when the tilt was pressed slightly backward. This made the business of "shutting" the cloches considerably faster.

Specific styles of tools were also used in the French gardening system. Shovels, forks, spades, hoes, rakes, and other tools were all needed, though the fork got the most use. The French gardeners used tools with relatively long, smooth handles varying in length from 3½ to 6 feet, which made it easier to throw manure or soil to any distance or height. Watering cans were also developed for ease and speed of use, and special pack baskets evolved for carrying manure and soil along the narrow paths where wheelbarrows could not go (see Figure 32).

One of the most notable aspects of the French system was the large areas that were made into hotbeds with fermenting horse manure. The way in which the hotbeds themselves were made de-

pended on the condition of the soil, the desired temperature of the beds, and the season of the year. No matter what the situation, though, it entailed moving and handling enormous quantities of manure as well as soil. Each successful grower had a method for efficiently preparing the beds to minimize the earth-moving involved.

Essentially the entire area was excavated to about 8 inches and filled with a specific mixture of composted manure and fresh manure with straw litter, to give off the proper warmth. The manure was piled to a depth of 9 to 18 inches depending on the amount and duration of heat required. It was trampled evenly, and covered with a few inches of soil. The frames were then placed on the beds and filled with a couple more inches of soil, which served to protect the plants from the hot manure and eliminate any drafts.

To give an idea of how this was done we will describe a simplified method for preparing a hypothetical 60-foot by 65-foot plot for hotbeds (see Figure 33). The first operation would be to mark out the area into 13-foot (the length of one frame)

**Figure 32**  *Basket for carrying manure on the narrow paths in a French garden—there being no room for wheelbarrows between beds. From* The French Garden *by C. D. McKay* (*London: Associated Newspapers, 1908*).

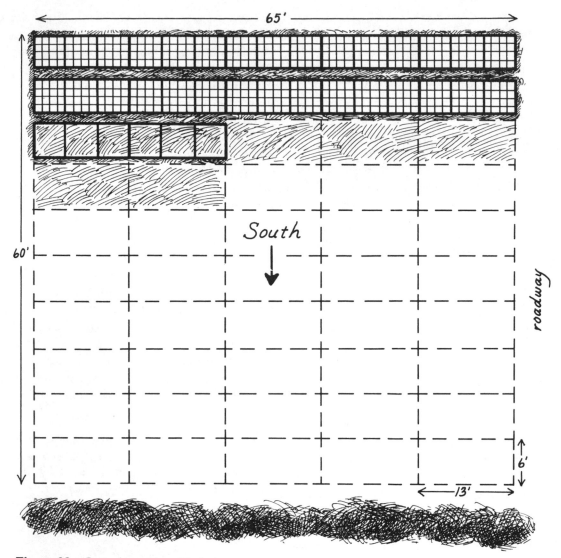

**Figure 33** *Preparing a plot of hotbeds.*

by 60-foot bands running north and south. Commonly five of these bands would be marked before including a north/south roadway in the layout. Next these bands would be divided into 6-foot sections (ten of them in this case) by lines running from east to west.

The digging would commence at the north end of the plot where a 6-foot by 65-foot trench would be opened along the markings. This would be dug to 8 inches deep and the soil transferred to the south end of the garden. If the soil was very heavy, this digging might be omitted to prevent water from collecting in the trench. Next, equal quantities of aged manure and fresh, hot manure with

straw litter would be mixed and placed in this trench. The fresh manure would be mixed with the old to give a steadier, longer supply of heat. The manure would be spread, firmed, and piled to the required depth, depending on the quantity of heat needed. Thicker beds were made in colder weather or for crops that required greater warmth. More manure would be used on wet ground, as it is generally colder. It is very important to compact this manure firmly and uniformly. Any inconsistency would encourage an uneven fermentation, and hence uneven heat and lopsided settling. To compact the manure it was beaten with the back of a spading fork and trodden down by foot. Once this was accomplished soil from the next 6-foot by 65-foot section was spread on top of the manure and firmed to a uniform depth of a couple of inches (see Figure 34). Then the frames were placed on top of the beds, centered from north to south in a long row, or range, approximately 4½ feet by 65 feet. More soil from the section directly south of this first range was spread and compacted inside the frames until there was a total of 5 to 6 inches over the manure. The lights were then put on the frames and more soil used to bank up the frames to keep out cold air. Thus the first range of lights was completed, and another 6-foot trench was ready to become the next range.

This is, of course, a simplified version of how the work might be done. Since this often had to be accomplished in the winter, provisions had to be made so that the soil would be neither frozen nor waterlogged; either of these conditions would have made it nearly impossible to make the hotbeds. To allow for this, the first trench on the north end of the garden was dug in the fall and the earth moved to the south end of the plot. In the remaining area soil was piled into ridges running north to south down the center of the bands. Ridging the soil helped it to drain well. Manure that had been collected through the summer was used to cover these ridges to ward off frost. Prior to making the beds, fresh manure would be collected and piled between the ridges where it would be convenient when the beds were made.

Once all the beds were made and the frames and lights in place, the beds were left to sit for a week or so before they were planted. After a few weeks when the beds began to cool, the aisles between the ranges were "lined" (filled) with more fresh hot manure "so that eventually all the frames look as if they were imbedded up to the lights in a sea of manure."[13]

Once the heat was exhausted from the manure, it was hardly useless. It was spread on open borders, on cloche beds, and over the manure in the hotbeds, where it made a very fertile growing medium. John Weathers describes the accumulation of this spent hotbed fuel in his book on French gardening.

> In some old Parisian gardens I visited, the manure of former years covered the original soil to a depth of two or three feet, and it almost felt as if one was walking on a velvet pile carpet. This old manure, decayed into fine particles, assumes a deeper and deeper tint with age, and yields up its fertilising foods under the influence of air, water, and heat for the benefit of crops grown upon it.[14]

Within the frames space was used as efficiently as possible. Several different vegetables that would not interfere with one another were grown in the same bed. Root crops were sown where they were to grow, while heading crops were transplanted at least once. One example of how this might work would be radishes and carrots sown together with lettuce seedlings. The radishes would be harvested while the carrots were still small, and the lettuce

[13] John Weathers. *French Market-Gardening* (London: John Murray, 1909), p. 23
[14] Weathers, p. 17.

**Figure 34** *Mixing soil and manure for under-glass crops. From* The Book of Market Gardening *by R. Lewis Castle (London: John Lane, 1906).*

would have grown to marketable size by the time the carrots needed more space. Sometimes the border of the bed would be planted with cauliflower seedlings, which would mature after the carrots were pulled. This sort of economy was practiced throughout the garden, and schemes included many different vegetables.

The whole system had been refined and specialized to the point that, despite the small scale of these market gardens, it was an entirely economical business. This is not to say that it wasn't hard work! The gardens were necessarily small because the labor and materials invested were very great and not at all practical on a large scale. Generally it was a family business, with all members helping in some way.

## THE FRENCH SYSTEM IN ENGLAND

By the beginning of the twentieth century this method had aroused interest in Great Britain, where, in spite of the general use of hotbeds and glass forcing structures, apparently nothing quite so systematic had developed. England was still importing fresh produce from France and Holland. One source claims that 24,000 to 30,000 crates of lettuce (each crate containing three dozen) came from France to the London market every week from just before Christmas until March. Other vegetables being imported from the French *maraîchers* included carrots, asparagus, turnips, radishes, and celeriac. Many people argued that it would be better to spend that money on early vegetables grown at home. This resulted in a party of gardeners from Evesham going to France and touring some of the intensive market gardens there to explore its feasibility for them.

The English growers were much impressed with what they saw, and in 1906 one of them, Mr. Indiens, hired a French expert to start a garden in Evesham on the French pattern. In the next year a French garden was started in Essex with the help of another French expert. "The press of the day, however, gave such optimistic and exaggerated reports relative to its possibilities for rapidly acquiring huge fortunes, that the system came into disrepute consequent upon the failure of inexperienced

growers. Several growers continued to work the system successfully, but the Great War cut short a good many promising ventures."[15]

World War I was not the only thing that cut the prospects of French intensive gardening short. As Dalziel O'Brien wrote:

Market gardening began with plenty of dung. Every city is ringed with the now built-over lands of men who sent their vegetables and fruit in and brought back the manure on the return load behind the horses ... the beginning of intensive horticulture under heavy pit lights with tiny panes of glass used this free manure, costing only loading time, as fuel in hotbeds as well. Some growers use artificials, with peat to supply the humus; some use chemically composted straw, and all of them pay heavily in direct cash and in labor for what their fathers and grandfathers had for free.[16]

The rise of the automobile and decline of the horse for transportation drastically altered the centuries-old balance of livery stable manure in exchange for intensively grown vegetables. Though cars began to come into use in the early 1900's, it was some years before the traffic in cities was mostly motor. In any case, this great change in transportation spelled eventual death to a system dependent on manure hotbeds to produce winter vegetables commercially.

While French gardening underwent both modifications and decline, intensive growing in general remained an economical way to supply local food for an urban population. This is especially true because the population density in these areas made the land too valuable to cultivate extensively. The future of large-scale manure hotbeds may have been doomed, but the use of glass was not. Glass remained in use for as long as it was necessary or profitable to produce food in an area or season where the climate prohibited growth in the open air.

In England the lights remained the most popular means of protection; the bell jars never caught

---

[15] C. P. Quarrel. *Intensive Salad Production* (London: Crosby, Lockwood and Sons Ltd., 1938), p. 69.

[16] R. Dalziel O'Brien. *Intensive Gardening* (London: Faber and Faber Ltd., 1956), p. 17.

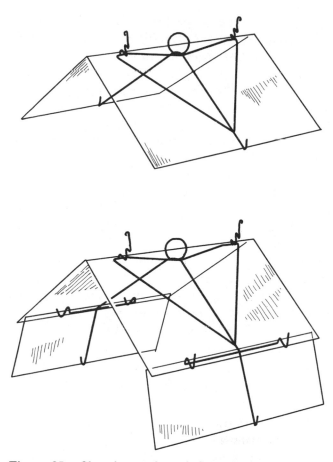

**Figure 35** *Chase barn and ten cloches.*

on in use as they had in France. Other protective devices were developed, such as the continuous cloche. This was invented by Major L. H. Chase and patented in 1912, and was much more versatile than the bell jar cloches (see Figure 35). The simpler version is a "tent" of two glass panes. This was improved by adding two more panes as vertical walls, the tent acting as a roof over this. The cloches could be used individually or could be arranged end to end to form long, miniature greenhouses covering entire rows of plants. This type of cloche was much lighter than the bell glasses and easier to repair, as broken panes could easily be replaced.

## DUTCH LIGHT GARDENING IN ENGLAND

In the early 1930's imports of foreign produce to Great Britain were restricted, greatly encouraging intensive market gardening there. At about the same time immigrants from Holland came to settle in Yorkshire, and apparently a number of them were growers. They brought their own equipment and methods for intensive cultivation, which spread fairly rapidly. The aspect of their system that seems to have been most valuable was their lights and the way in which they used them in the garden.

Dutch-style lights are made of one large pane of glass, rather than sixteen small ones as in the French lights. This allows a significantly increased amount of sunlight to pass through the frame to the plants. They covered slightly less area than French lights (the dimensions are 59 inches by 31¾ inches, roughly 5 feet by 2½ feet) and were lighter. These sashes were also an improvement over the standard English lights, which were a relatively large 4 feet by 6 feet, and very similar to the French type, made of a minimum of sixteen panes of glass. While the large piece of glass in the Dutch lights is a disadvantage in terms of breakage, the sash requires less painting and glazing. The Dutch lights were also readily adapted to rudimentary glass houses by wiring the lights to a simple framework. These houses were suited for such crops as tomatoes, which were too tall to grow in the low frames.

The Dutch growers in England adopted double span frames for their lights rather than single frames. These facilitated a less intensive cropping system than the French gardeners used, called "alternative frame cropping." The Dutch system is still in use in Great Britain today. In this system the lights are used alternately on one range of frames and then on the adjacent ones, switching back and forth (see Figure 36). This is coordinated with the crops growing in the frames. It means that the ground is exposed to the weather after

**Figure 36** *A double span frame (used here for starting tomato plants). From* Garden Farming *by Lee Cleveland Corbett (Boston: Ginn & Co., 1913).*

every crop, and that the grower is not in a frantic rush to prepare the beds between crops. It is a system that makes maximum use of the glass involved, for when a crop under glass is harvested, the lights can be immediately transferred to a bed already prepared and planted.

Unlike the French system, where the soil was soon covered with a depth of manure, nearly eliminating any soil fertility problems, Dutch growers with a limited manure supply had to choose soil more carefully. This was especially true in a situation where the ground was covered with glass, limiting the weathering effects of freezing and thawing, wetting and drying. Under these circumstances it was particularly important to have a soil that was naturally loose and well drained, without being dry.

Manures, of course, were needed to supply fertility and humus. However, while one writer advises that initially a French garden may require 500 tons of manure per acre, the recommendation for Dutch light gardens averages 50 tons per acre. These are very broad figures, and the qualities of both soils and manures vary widely. For comparison, current American books inform that 10 to 15 tons of manure per acre is an average application. (This is for nonintensive use.) This gives an idea of the relation of intensive cropping to intensive manuring, as well as giving some concept of the quantity of manure needed for heat, as opposed to fertility, in French gardening.

## FORCING AND MARKET GARDENING IN NORTH AMERICA

In the United States there were also intensive market gardens to supply large cities and towns with vegetables. Writing in the 1830's, Loudon commented that

> Market gardens are not yet established in America on a large scale, but there are numerous small ones; and in the neighborhood of all the larger towns, as in the neighborhood of Liverpool in England, the superfluous produce of private gardens is sent to market.[17]

[17] Loudon. *An Encyclopedia of Gardening*, p. 339.

There were many market gardens in the New York area, said to supply Fulton Market with excellent fruits and vegetables. Boston residents also had a wide variety of choice produce at the Faneuil Hall Market. As has always been the case, commercial production of vegetables and fruits was restricted to the environs of towns large enough to support such enterprises. Naturally gardeners could not afford to subject their produce to more travel than was necessary. This was truer then than it is today because of poor refrigeration and because so many vegetable varieties have been developed for their firmness or hard rinds, which are an advantage in shipping. This meant that market gardens thrived mostly in the already urban Northeast, in spite of the less-than-ideal climate. American growers, like their European counterparts, used hotbeds and cold frames to produce the out-of-season vegetables that commanded higher prices.

By 1850 industrial development in northern urban areas was changing the agriculture of that area by increasing the demand for everything, including vegetables and fruits. Production in this populous area turned to more intensive means, while things like grain, which were cultivated extensively and could tolerate shipping, were grown in the Midwest (see Figures 37–39). In the Northeast, as land became more valuable, "Farmers were tiling their wet areas. Land not suitable for intensive use was being abandoned, and farmers not able to adapt themselves to the more intensive and capitalistic type of farming were moving into industry or migrating west to farm in their old way there."[18]

As the Northeast became more industrial, the population changed "from a producing to a consuming one."[19] A middle class emerged, able to afford the more expensive forced vegetables. Market gardening grew accordingly.

> ... the value of orchard and garden products for 1859 reveals that four states in which industry and urban growth were most concentrated—Massachusetts, New York, New Jersey, and Pennsylvania—

[18] Paul W. Gates. *The Farmer's Age: Agriculture 1815–1860.* (New York: Harper and Row, 1960), p. 269.
[19] Lee Cleveland Corbett. *Garden Farming* (Boston: Ginn and Co., 1913), p. 2.

**Figure 37** *Cold frames in American market gardens used for growing cucumbers.* From Garden Farming *by Lee Cleveland Corbett (Boston: Ginn & Co., 1913).*

**Figure 38** *American market gardeners made easily movable frames to carry glass lights by constructing only the paths. Older, experienced gardeners much preferred this construction.* From Starting Early Vegetable and Flowering Plants Under Glass *by Charles Nissley (New York: Orange Judd, 1929).*

**Figure 39** *Rye straw mats are used in American gardens to protect frame crops from cold weather.* From Starting Early Vegetable and Flowering Plants Under Glass *by Charles Nissley (New York: Orange Judd, 1929).*

plus Ohio, constituted an orchard and truck garden belt. These five states of the thirty-three in the Union produced 47 percent of the value of fruits and vegetables the country yielded.[20]

Truck gardening, however, differed from traditional market gardening. The fact that vegetables were transported, initially by steamer and later by railroad, meant that they were grown farther from their markets. Because of this growers could take advantage of cheaper land in more rural areas and

milder climates farther south. These conditions did not require an intensive use of the land or a serious forcing culture. The progress of the season from Florida northward, combined with refrigeration and fast freight, served to supply large cities with fresh produce throughout the entire year.

"Yet," wrote Corbett in 1913, "it [truck gardening] has not discouraged the development of the forcing industry, which has for a number of years been an important branch of market gardening in the vicinity of the large northern cities."[21] Because

[20] Gates, p. 269.

[21] Corbett, p. 3.

Figure 40 *A forcing house and frames covered with glass lights. Note the coverings of burlap coated with linseed oil made from old fertilizer bags on frames in the left foreground. From* Starting Early Vegetable and Flowering Plants Under Glass *by Charles Nissley (New York: Orange Judd, 1929).*

of the expense of covering beds with glass and heating them, cropping was necessarily intensive. This industry was, in the early 1900's, most highly developed in the Boston area. Manure, or hot water or steam flowing through pipes, supplied heat for hotbeds. Glass forcing houses were heated too so that tomatoes, cucumbers, and lettuce could be grown through the winter (see Figure 40). In milder areas cold frames were used in market gardens, though hotbeds were used for starting seedlings (see Figures 41 and 42). In other areas frames were used, covered with "muslins." These consisted of a lightweight, standard-size (3 feet by 6 feet) framework with unbleached muslin stretched over each side of it to form a sort of double "glazed" effect. These were all that was needed for protection in southern sections of the country.

Near Montreal melons were raised for market in

a way more reminiscent of the French gardens near Paris. There was a large, green-fleshed melon known as the Montreal Market. Hotbeds were made with an 18-inch depth of fermenting manure in which the heat was allowed to temper for a week or so. Then melon plants were transplanted into the frames, two seedlings under each sash, and the sash was covered on cold nights. The melon plants grew until nearly mature before the frames were removed. Under each fruit was placed a shingle or flat stone to keep it off the ground, and the melons were turned regularly for uniform ripening.

Our urban centers are no longer surrounded by small-scale, intensively cultivated market gardens, for fast, economical transportation has totally changed the commercial production of vegetables in our country. However, because of the rising

Figure 41 *Sweet potatoes in cold frames. From* Garden Farming *by Lee Cleveland Corbett (Boston: Ginn & Co., 1913).*

Figure 42 *Tomato seedlings in cold frames. From* Starting Early Vegetable and Flowering Plants Under Glass *by Charles Nissley (New York: Orange Judd, 1929).*

price of fuel needed to ship vegetables in the current system, small growers may again find it economical to use intensive methods to supply local markets.

Throughout history there have been various reasons to use intensive methods, from raised beds for solving drainage problems to cropping procedures that made the most efficient possible use of space. Reasons have not changed, and gardeners today are beginning to find the same benefits from gardening intensively as did their predecessors. Though materials have changed, the methods that were used in gardens of the past are of vital use to us today.

# 2

## SOIL IN THE INTENSIVE GARDEN

Paul Doscher

A RICH, dynamic, and healthy soil is a key to the success of any garden. Any method of growing plants will produce good results if the soil is good. But with intensive gardening the density of cropping and constant use of the soil mean that a rich soil resource is absolutely critical. With it production and plant health can be virtually assured. Without it, failure and disappointment are almost certain.

### WHAT IS SOIL?

Obviously, if soil is so important, it is a good idea for every intensive gardener to understand what soil really is. Soil is an "ecosystem," a series of interacting groups of organisms and all the environmental factors that affect them. It is not only the particles of rock we call clay, silt, or sand, but all the decaying organic matter, animals, fungi, bacteria, and plants that inhabit this underground world. Factors we don't normally consider part of soil—air, water, sun, heat, and cold—are also integral to the function and life of the soil ecosystem.

Under natural conditions soil is constantly changing. To the naked eye this change is imperceptible. Yet, when we look close enough, it becomes evident that the activity in the soil is as diverse and complex as any we can observe above ground. At any one point varieties of processes are going on just below the surface of the ground, including weathering of rock. The action of air, water, cold, and heat are constantly working to pulverize rock material. This occurs both above the ground, where rock is exposed to the elements of weather, and below ground, where complicated chemical and physical actions break apart the bedrock well below the topsoil. But environmental factors are not the only ones that act to "weather" rock. Such plants as lichens, mosses, and liverworts produce acids as waste products. These acids dissolve rocks, causing small particles to fall off. Below ground, plant roots creep into rock crevices and expand, causing the rock to break apart. In rich organic soils tiny particles of rock are constantly being broken down by the action of organic acids produced by soil bacteria, fungi, and small animals.

Life within the soil ecosystem is extremely im-

22

**Figure 43** *A freshly built bed of soil. Any method of growing plants will produce good results if the soil is good.*

portant (see Figure 44). In fact, without the thousands of kinds of organisms inhabiting it soil is nothing more than "dirt." The most obvious soil organisms are plants. Plant roots not only break apart rock into smaller particles, but they also excrete substances which in turn dissolve soil particles into mineral nutrients. Most important, all plant material ultimately becomes dead organic matter, which, if allowed to return into the soil, becomes the food source of microscopic soil life.

Dead organic matter is quickly attacked and is gradually consumed by thousands of bacteria, fungi, insects, and other tiny animals. In some fertile forest soils the quantity of soil bacteria alone is estimated to weigh as much as 5,600 pounds per acre. In agricultural soils the quantity is lower, but it tips the scales at a quarter to a half ton per acre. Bacteria perform many important functions, including the decomposition of plant tissues into minerals, the fixing or absorption of nitrogen from the air, and the production of wastes, which become food for other soil organisms. Generally, soil bacteria are highly beneficial. Unfortunately, some are the sources of harmful crop diseases.

Fungi perform many of the same tasks as bacteria. Fungi such as mushrooms, which act to break down organic matter into mineral nutrients and humus, are called saprophytes. They attack even

**Figure 44** *Common soil organisms.*

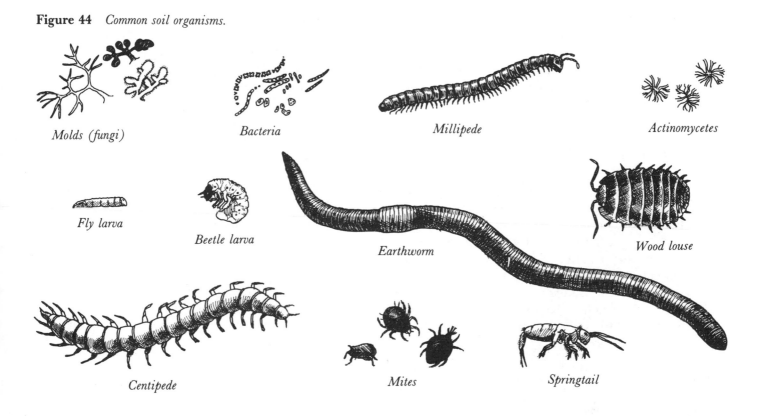

Molds (fungi)

Bacteria

Millipede

Actinomycetes

Fly larva

Beetle larva

Earthworm

Wood louse

Centipede

Mites

Springtail

the most decay-resistant materials, tree bark, for instance, and recycle their components back into the soil. Fungi are also the janitors of the soil, working to clean up the waste products and bodies of dead bacteria.

Another group, actinomycetes, are half fungi, half bacteria-like organisms that are present in all soils in small quantities. They do the same work as fungi, but grow best in warmer environments. The compost pile is a favorite home for actinomycetes, for they thrive in the warmth created by heat-producing bacteria.

The natural cultivators of soil are invertebrate animals. These creatures, without skeletons or with external skeletons, are the most numerous and successful group of animals ever to exist on earth. Many of them spend all or part of their lives in the soil. Mites, ants, millipedes, centipedes, sow bugs, and many insects burrow through the soil in search of food. In the process they create minute channels which aid the passage of air, water, and plant roots. When these creatures die, their bodies serve as food for bacteria and fungi.

The most famous soil-cultivator is the earthworm. There are many species of earthworms, all of which are important to some degree in soil cultivation. Some types are prolific producers of "castings" (excrement rich in minerals and plant nutrients). Earthworms, like other soil organisms, feed almost exclusively upon dead organic matter.

Other wormlike animals that benefit soils are the nematodes. They are very small creatures, often microscopic, many of which are helpful in soil building and aeration. Not all nematodes are beneficial. Some are parasites on plant roots, and some are spreaders of fungal diseases, but these types are found in non-harmful quantities in healthy soils.

The smallest group of soil organisms, but by far the most noticeable, is the larger animals. Burrowing moles, mice, gophers, voles, squirrels, woodchucks, and others carry the cultivation process to the extreme. Their activity is of great benefit in mixing and aerating soils, but in gardens where plants lack deep and extensive root systems animal tunnels are a nuisance and can do great damage to crops. Nonetheless, larger animals are an important part of the soil ecosystem, and in their natural environment do much to help build fertile soils.

The importance of the roles of all these creatures cannot be underestimated. They play an essential role, in combination with the processes and elements of the environment, in assuring the continued growth of the soil ecosystem. As a general rule, the more variety of organisms within a soil system, the better. This is because nature promotes diversity as a means of creating stability—survival of the system. In diverse systems there is such a multitude of organisms at work that if one disappears or is eliminated, its individual loss is not catastrophic to the whole system.

Diversity of life is what builds rich soils in which plants grow strong and healthy. A soil that has abundant organic matter, bacteria, fungi, and other animals, plenty of air, water, and light, cannot help but produce profuse plant growth.

## WHAT MAKES GOOD GARDEN SOIL?

Good garden soil contains all the same components as good natural soil in a virgin forest or prairie. The differences are that nature takes thousands of years to build rich deep soils; the intensive gardener needs to create them in only a few years. Additionally, the intensive garden is covered much more densely with fast-growing plants than are most forest soils or even conventional garden soils. Thus, all the essential life and minerals in soil must be compacted into a smaller space than they might normally occupy.

Creating the proper conditions for a successful garden requires some manipulation of the natural soil. This is particularly true in areas where the activities of man have caused the natural topsoil to be eroded or depleted, leaving only a bare skin of rich organic matter on top of mineral, relatively lifeless subsoil. Achieving the proper conditions will benefit any garden, but they are even more important in intensive gardens.

### Aeration

Plants and soil organisms need air to breath. Plant roots absorb oxygen from the air and give off carbon dioxide; they will suffocate in the absence of air. (Above ground, portions of plants do the opposite; they absorb carbon dioxide and give off oxygen.) Soil animals, like any other creatures, must breathe oxygen. In dense or compacted soil the tiny spaces between particles are too small to allow free flow of air, and plant growth and soil functions suffer.

## Water Drainage

Much of the water that falls as rain percolates downward through pore spaces between larger soil particles. This "gravitational" water eventually flows into the underground water table. As it flows downward it is replaced by fresh air from above. In heavy clay soils, which have no large spaces or pores, water does not drain quickly enough, and plants can literally drown during extended rainy periods.

## Water Retention

Not all water flows downward as gravitational water. Some remains in the very tiny spaces between smaller soil particles or is captured through the spongelike action of humus. This is capillary water and is the source of moisture for most plant growth. A good soil is both well drained of gravitational water and has the ability to retain capillary water. Although sandy soils have good drainage, sand particles are relatively large and do not create enough of the small spaces necessary to hold capillary water. This makes sandy soils very drought susceptible.

## Balanced Nutrients

Nutrients are the source of plant growth. They are mineral substances consumed by plants to help create all the various plant tissues. These mineral substances are found in all soils in varying amounts and forms.

Just as humans need a balanced diet containing essential proteins, fats, and carbohydrates, along with vitamins and minerals, plants require a balanced supply of nitrogen, potassium, phosphorus, calcium, sulfur, magnesium, and many other substances. Different plants have varying nutrient re-

quirements, but it is generally true that if a soil has an overall balance of these nutrients, it will produce good crops. On the other hand, too little of an important plant nutrient will result in a deficiency leading to poor health and slowed growth. Too much of a plant nutrient can be equally harmful, resulting in poor utilization of other nutrients or even crop failure.

## Balanced pH

"Potential hydrogen" (pH), is a measure of the acidity and alkalinity of any substance. It is measured on a scale of 0 to 14, with 0 being extremely acid and 14 extremely alkaline. Seven is the neutral point. Most garden plants grow best in soils with a pH of 6.0 to 7.0. Although specific plants like more acid or alkaline conditions, the best garden soil falls within this range (see Figure 45). Phosphorus, also many trace elements, are most available to plants in slightly acid soil conditions. More acidic conditions cause certain plant nutrients to be tightly attached to the soil, so they cannot be absorbed by plant roots. In alkaline soils some nutrients combine through chemical bonds into substances unusable by plants.

## Plentiful Humus and Soil Life

Humus is a substance consisting of fine particles of organic matter, the end product of decomposition. In comparison with fresh organic material it is relatively resistant to further decomposition by bacteria and fungi. It is the most important component of good soil.

Humus is porous and lets air and light into the soil. It tends to increase the number and size of pore spaces in heavy soils, thereby improving drainage and at the same time acting like a sponge to hold capillary water. Since humus is the product of organic decomposition, during which mineral nutrients are slowly released into the soil, efforts to increase humus almost always result in improved nutrient balance. Lastly, humus acts as a "buffer" to help hold pH close to neutral (or slightly acid), reducing the need for other actions to correct pH balance.

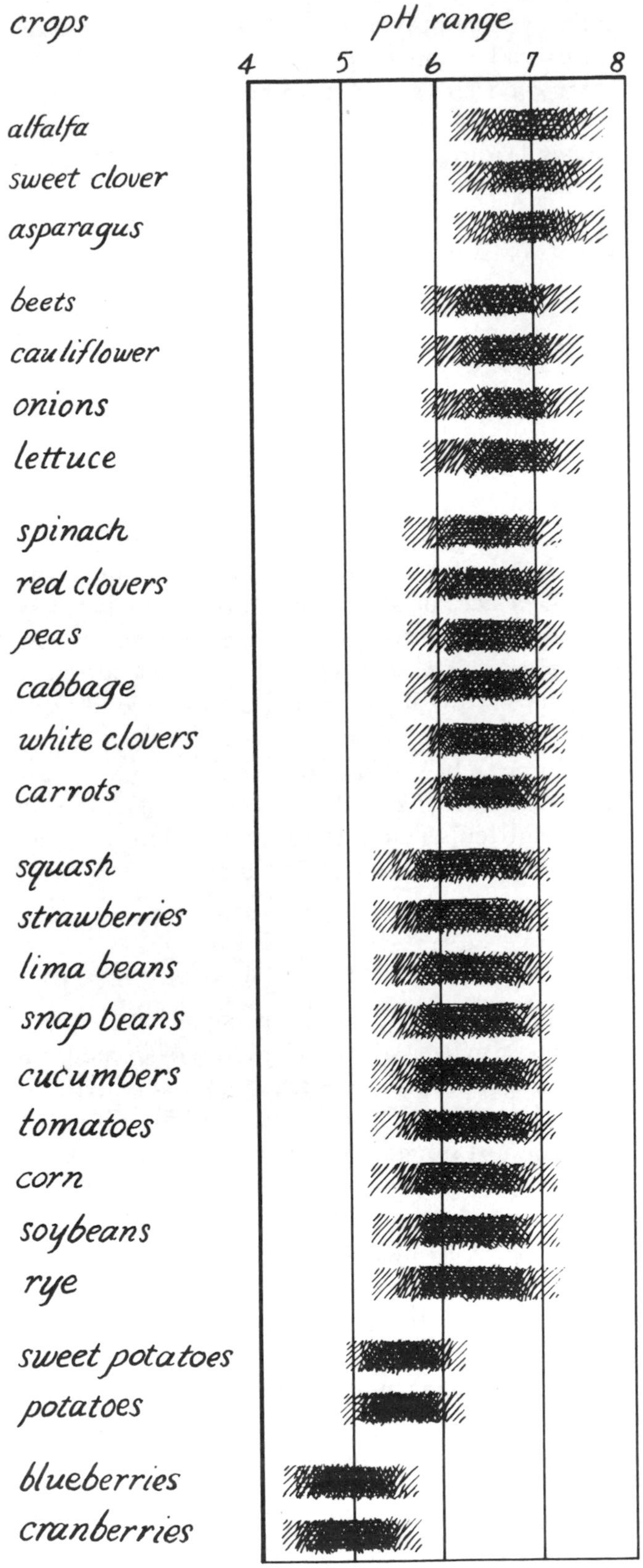

crops
pH range

4 5 6 7 8

alfalfa
sweet clover
asparagus

beets
cauliflower
onions
lettuce

spinach
red clovers
peas
cabbage
white clovers
carrots

squash
strawberries
lima beans
snap beans
cucumbers
tomatoes
corn
soybeans
rye

sweet potatoes
potatoes

blueberries
cranberries

**Figure 45**  *The pH preferences of common crops.*

A full diversity of soil life is necessary to create humus, and the process of creating humus is just as important as the humus itself. The activity of microorganisms in breaking down organic substances releases not only the mineral nutrients needed by plants but creates an environment where other organisms can live, many of which have important roles to play in providing additional nutrients and minerals. This constant and gradual release of nutrients and minerals provides the most beneficial conditions for healthy plant growth.

The best intensive garden soils are built with the goal of achieving all of the above conditions. The soil that results is dark in color, loose in texture (it is easy to scoop up a handful without a digging tool), holds capillary water (stays damp just an inch or two below the surface), never has standing water on it (even after heavy rains), and rarely requires massive infusions of fertilizers or pH adjustment. The major requirement the soil makes of the gardener is to keep it fed with regular supplies of organic matter.

## BUILDING INTENSIVE GARDEN SOIL

It is a lucky gardener who can begin an intensive garden in a place where the soil is so rich, dark, loose, and dynamic that no further soil building is necessary. Most of us are faced with the knowledge of what our soil should be and with the realization that it isn't even close to what we'd like it to be. After this realization comes the determination to "dig in" and start the laborious and time-consuming process of soil building.

Unfortunately, many gardeners make their first mistake right here. They rush out and buy soil amendments or hunt for the nearest source of manure without first taking the time to discover what it is their soil really needs. Although dumping quantities of high-priced organic amendments or fresh manure on a poor soil will probably not make it worse, it may not make it much better.

What every new gardener, and especially every new intensive gardener, should do first is take some time to know the soil. You can learn quite a bit by simply observing soil and determining its strengths and weaknesses through a modest testing program. Then you can work to solve the problems in a direct way without also putting a lot of effort into improving conditions that are already good. For example, if a soil is poorly drained but high in humus and nutrients, adding lots of fresh manure or other organic matter may help, but the problem might be solved more easily by digging a drainage ditch and adding some sand. What is really needed is a way to get rid of the excess water.

The types of soil problems most often faced by the intensive gardener fall into the following four categories:

1. Poor soil texture (drainage and aeration)
2. Inadequate nutrient supply
3. Inadequate humus content
4. Unbalanced pH

All of these problems can be solved with some planning, some understanding, and some manual labor. In most cases solutions need not involve spending large amounts of money on exotic soil amendments or fertilizers. Here's how to deal with the problems you are likely to find in each category.

### 1. Improving Soil Texture

Most of the bulk of soil is nothing more than minute bits of rock. They range in size from large grains of sand visible to the naked eye to microscopically small particles of silt and clay so small as to appear to form a solid mass. Each has a distinct and profound effect upon soil quality, which is commonly called soil texture.

During the last century the Soil Conservation Service of the U.S. Department of Agriculture has surveyed most of the nation, testing soils for their texture and other qualities. Soils have been classified into distinct categories and their individual characteristics described. Information on local soils is available to the public at any county office of the SCS. It is useful, although not generally essential, for you to obtain this information before selecting a place to build an intensive garden. If you have a large plot of land, it can steer you away from spots which may look good on the surface but just below ground have impervious hardpan, high water table, bedrock, or heavy clay. On the other hand, if you already have a garden spot or only one choice of a place to put it, a soil survey is nothing more than interesting reading.

What a soil survey and your own inspection will tell you is the density and texture of your soil. It will probably fall into one of the following categories:

1. *Gravelly sand.* Extremely coarse particles, which make for a very well-drained but droughty soil that loses nutrients very quickly.
2. *Sandy loam.* Coarse particles, which are well drained, droughty in dry spells, lose nutrients quickly, and will not form clods when squeezed in the hand.
3. *Loams and silt loams.* Medium-grained soils, which are moderately well drained but have enough fine particles and organic matter to hold capillary water. These are the most fertile of natural soils and are usually found in rivers valleys or flat plains. These soils form clods when squeezed, but the clods break apart easily when handled.
4. *Clay Loams.* Fine-grained soils, which are slow to drain but have moderate organic matter that keeps them from becoming too easily saturated. They can be very fertile, because fine-grained soils hold nutrients well. They form compact clods when squeezed in the hand, but break apart easily when dropped.
5. *Heavy clay.* These are extremely fine-grained soils, which appear greasy when wet. They are often poorly drained and aerated. Heavy clays hold nutrients so tightly that plants often have trouble obtaining nourishment. They compact easily into bricklike masses, which can be broken up only by the use of tools or tillers. Dried clods can become as hard as rocks.

Obviously there are numerous variations and combinations of these basic types. Of the five the most desirable are loams and silt loams. They have an excellent combination of aeration, drainage, organic content, water retention, and nutrient holding ability. But what do you do if you have a less desirable soil? The following rules of thumb should be your guide:

1. *Sandy soils.* Turning in any organic material will add to the water holding capacity of the soil. The sandier the soil the more organic material it will take. It may require that 3 to 6 inches of material be added to the top few inches of soil for three to four years. The key is to create a sponge effect. Adding loam may help, but fine particles easily slip downward between grains of sand and can be lost to the subsoil. Building humus content will also help the soil hold nutrients.

2. *Clay soils.* If the soil is also poorly drained, look around first for the slope of the land, then dig a drainage trench (with gently sloping sides) 1 to 2 feet deep in a direction that will carry water away from your garden. Next, loosen the soil with a rototiller or garden fork to a depth of about 12 inches, or to the level where mineral subsoil begins. One to 4 inches of coarse sand can be added over the entire bed to provide immediate loosening, but organic material is essential for long-term improvement (see Figures 46–48). Humus will increase the porosity of the soil over time, but it cannot create instant results. Adding too much organic material at one time can result in a long decomposition process that will tie up essential plant nutrients.

**Figure 46** *Sand and compost added to bed before preparation. Note the finished bed in the foreground.*

In either case, these rules should be followed if possible: (1) Add well-composted or rotten material if planting is to follow within a month of soil preparation, and (2) if fresh material must be used, use it either in the fall when no further cropping is anticipated or when the soil is to be left fallow for longer than a month. The exception to this rule is when green manures are used in spring. With green manures, allow at least three weeks between turning in and planting of crops.

Your ultimate objective is to produce a loose, crumbly-textured soil which forms easily broken clods when squeezed in the hand.

In most places topsoil is shallower than the 18-inch depth that is most desirable for intensive gardening. This can prove to be a problem if the subsoil below is hard clay or so densely compacted that it constricts root growth. But before undertaking a laborious effort to break up the subsoil consider the following (and refer to Figure 49):

1. In climates where winter temperatures drop consistently below 0°F (−15°C) frost penetrates deeply into the ground. In beds not covered by glazing or mulch, freezing is a major cause of subsoil loosening. This is a natural process, which can provide enough cracks and pores in subsoils to allow considerable root penetration. We observed this effect in an experiment conducted in our Hancock, N.H. garden, with beds that were double dug (double digging is a method by which the topsoil is temporarily removed in small sections, allowing the subsoil to be loosened, resulting in loose soil to a depth of as much as 2 feet), double-dug beds yielded no significant improvement over undug subsoil in other beds. In both cases the subsoil is a heavy clay about 16 to 18 inches below the surface.

2. In temperate climates earthworms burrow deep into the subsoil to avoid winter cold. During a recent fall we removed a full 10 inches of topsoil from a one-year-old bed. We then observed that at the interface between the humus-rich topsoil and mineral subsoil the density of earthworms was almost 5 per square foot. The worms were apparently moving downward into the subsoil as the soil temperatures dropped. Our intention had been to loosen the subsoil with the rototiller, and in doing so we discovered an amazingly large quantity of earthworms even farther down. It is

**Figure 47** *Sand and compost are turned into an intensive bed with a spading fork. Note that this bed is only 2½ feet wide and can be straddled while working.*

**Figure 48** *Freshly prepared beds in the garden of Paul and Debbie Doscher in New Hampshire. The ultimate objective is to produce a loose, crumbly soil that forms easily broken clods when squeezed in the hand.*

doubtful if we will ever bother to go through all the grief of double digging or tilling the subsoil again with this army of cultivators doing it for us.

3. If you have such an impervious subsoil that even worms don't work through it, or if you live in a moderate climate where freezing fails to penetrate the topsoil, consider loosening the subsoil. A number of subsoil loosening methods are described in Chapter 4.

One last comment about soil texture. Once you have obtained the conditions you want, don't stop adding organic matter. It is possible to reduce the additions somewhat, but since humus does decay over time, adding no organic matter at all will eventually put you right back where you started.

## 2. Balancing and Adding Plant Nutrients

Water is the most essential plant nutrient and accounts for 90 percent of the substance of non-woody plants. Following water in importance are carbon, hydrogen, and oxygen, which plants obtain from air and water. These three are the building blocks of photosynthesis and comprise most of the solid material in plant tissues.

The mineral nutrients gardeners are most con-

**Figure 49** *Earthworms are able assistants in loosening subsoils in most climates. Earthworms often make double digging or other laborious subsoil loosening techniques unnecessary.*

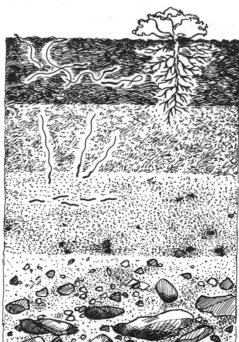

Earthworms spend most of their time in topsoil feeding on organic matter

But when winter approaches they move downward to stay below the level of freezing

and during the cold weather "hibernate" at depths down to 6 feet! They are even able to penetrate through dense hardpan layers

Topsoil high in organic material

Loosened subsoil mostly mineral matter

Unloosened subsoil mineral matter (occasionally with an impervious "hardpan" layer)

Bedrock, glacial material mostly rock

cerned about actually make up only a tiny percentage of the dry weight of plants. Even so, they are critical to growth, flowering and fruiting. Today thirteen nutrients have been proven to be necessary in plants, although it is likely that scientists will add more to this list in the future. They fall into two categories: macronutrients, which plants require in relatively large amounts, and micronutrients (trace minerals), which are used in very minute amounts.

The macronutrients are nitrogen, phosphorus, potassium, calcium, magnesium, and sulfur. Micronutrients are iron, boron, manganese, zinc, molybdenum, copper, and chlorine.

It is not possible to determine accurately how much of any nutrient is present in soil without chemical testing. This can be done with moderately successful results using one of the better commercially available soil test kits (see Figure 50). (It is not advisable to buy a very inexpensive test kit; the results you will get can be very inaccurate.) A more precise test can be performed by sending samples to a professional laboratory or the Agricultural Extension Service lab in your state.

We recommend testing soil regularly during the first few years of intensive gardening. Nutrients are depleted much more rapidly in intensive beds, and knowing how much of a nutrient is present is essential to determining the amount to add. Without testing you will be using the "shotgun" approach, and it is possible that a lot of your ammunition will be wasted or that you may not be adding the right nutrients.

Generally, as soil tilth improves and humus content increases, frequent soil testing becomes less important. As mentioned earlier, nutrient levels tend to fluctuate less in organic soils, since the decomposition process yields a continual supply of most nutrients.

Do not test soil immediately after adding fresh organic matter. The nutrient material in fresh matter is attacked by soil life and consumed in their digestive systems for as long as a month. Testing soil at this time would provide false results which do not reflect the ultimate availability of the nutrients once decomposition is complete.

Testing is best done in early spring, before planting or fertilizing, and in fall before planting winter or cover crops. Some gardeners also test in mid-summer, but this is not essential. Always be sure to follow the instructions that come with the soil testing kit to get accurate results.

Of the macronutrients, nitrogen, phosphorus, and potassium (abbreviated NPK) must be replenished regularly as part of the soil-building program. Calcium, magnesium, and sulfur are equally important to plant growth, but are usually abundant in soils or need only occasional replenishment.

*Nitrogen.* Nitrogen is the most plentiful component of air (77.5 percent), but in its gaseous form it is inert and unusable by plants or animals. In its mineral forms (ammonia and nitrates) it is a key element in the production of chlorophyll, the substance that is the basis of photosynthesis. It is also necessary for the production of plant proteins and amino acids. Because plants prefer to use nitrogen as nitrates, and nitrates are soluble in water, this important nutrient is often in short supply in garden soil. It can be present in adequate quantities in the beginning of the gardening season, only to be leached away by rainwater and gradually used up by densely cropped plants. To minimize this problem it is recommended that nitrogen be supplied to the soil in the form of organic matter. The slow decomposition of the material releases nitrates over the course of many months, providing better and more consistent plant growth. If mid-

**Figure 50** *A good soil kit includes chemicals for conducting tests for nitrate, phosphate, potassium, pH, and humus.*

season nitrogen "boosting" is necessary, a liquid tea can be made from compost, manure, fish emulsion, or certain soil amendments. Another approach is to "side-dress" with a mulch of compost, grass clippings or other nitrogen-rich material.

For intensive gardens the best sources of nitrogen are rotted manure, compost, and green manures (see Figures 51 and 52). These materials (except green manures) will provide the most nitrogen if they are stored under cover. Rainwater rapidly diminishes the fertilizer value of uncovered materials. You may choose to look into some of the products made from human sewage or the sludge from sewage treatment plants. They can provide substantial quantities of nitrogen and other nutrients, but you must be sure that they are tested and free of toxic metals and chemicals before you use them in the garden. Unless the material is frequently tested or certified safe, it is best to stay away from these substances. This is unfortunate, since using human waste would be a logical way to complete the nutrient cycle from soil to plant to man and back to the soil. Perhaps one day we will legislate that no industrial or toxic wastes can be dumped into our municipal sewers, and this resource will become safe for use in producing food. But until that day BE CAUTIOUS!

**Figure 52** *Green manure crops hold nutrients during periods when beds are not in use, returning them to the soil after being turned under.*

*Phosphorus.* Phosphorus is used by plants in the form of phosphate ($PO_4$). It is important in the basic process of plant growth and cell division, and it is essential for healthy seedling growth, root growth, flowering, and fruit development.

Phosphate is water soluble, but in most soils it is greatly attracted to tiny soil particles and does not percolate out in rainwater. The major loss of phosphates comes primarily from its use by plants and the harvesting of fruits, which concentrate this nutrient.

The best way to add phosphorus to soil is through organic material. Most compost and manures contain a fair amount of phosphorus. If this proves to be inadequate, then it is economical to add phosphorus in the form of ground rock phosphate. Added in the rock form, the phosphate will gradually break down in the soil, making it unnecessary to add more for up to three years.

*Potassium.* This nutrient is particularly important because it is a basic catalyst for many plant functions. It must be present for plants to manufacture sugars, proteins, and amino acids, even though it is usually not present in these substances. It is also critical to the flowering process. It is usually added to the soil in the form of potash,

**Figure 51** *Legumes are plants which host nitrogen-fixing bacteria on their roots. Using legumes as cover/green manure crops can add substantial amounts of nitrogen to the soil. These blackeyed peas have well-developed nitrogen nodules on the roots.*

31

which is found in wood ashes, granite dust, or greensand. It is not plentiful in manures, except cow manure, and it leaches out quite quickly. For suburban gardeners the best source of potassium can be freshly cut grass clippings. Potassium is concentrated in the leaves of plants, and grass is especially good for this. The clippings can be used as mulch, and the potassium will leach out of the leaves into the soil during rainstorms.

*Calcium.* This plentiful element has many uses in plants, but its most notable use is in the formation of cell walls. As in animals, calcium provides strength to the skeleton of plants. In soils where limestone is the parent material calcium is usually abundant and does not need to be added. In other places calcium is added during the occasional process of adjusting pH with the use of ground limestone.

Only rarely is this element a limiting factor in good plant growth. It is abundant and finds its way into the soil in many of the other fertilizers used to provide nitrogen, phosphorus, and potassium.

*Magnesium.* Magnesium is another critical component of chlorophyll and is part of the chemical structure of amino acids, vitamins, sugars, and plant fats. Sandy soils, particularly along the Atlantic Coast, appear to be severely deficient in magnesium. Most other soils are naturally rich in this element. Where it must be added, the best sources are raw rock phosphate and dolomitic limestone.

*Sulfur.* Sulfur is used by plants in the manufacture of vitamins, particularly the B vitamins. It is such a plentiful nutrient that only in extremely unusual circumstances is the addition of sulfur required. Perhaps one of the few positive effects of the burning of fossil fuels is the contribution it makes to preventing sulfur depletion in soils. Sulfur is a major contaminant in most fossil fuels, and when we burn them, sulfur dioxide is released into the atmosphere. It is then washed out as acid rain (in the form of sulfuric acid) and ends up back on the ground. Of course, if it lands on cars, houses, and other man-made objects, it causes corrosion, and in streams and lakes it can seriously affect fish life. But in soils the only apparent effect is the reduction of pH. This assures that in most of the

U.S. there is no deficiency of sulfur for plant growth.

There is considerable controversy over the acid rain problem. It is definitely a form of environmental pollution, and many scientists are very concerned about its effect in disrupting natural ecosystems. However, in agricultural soils the only noticeable problem seems to be the increased need to adjust pH. However, further research may reveal other negative effects, and in general we consider acid rain a problem that should be solved, not tolerated. If and when the day comes that acid rain is substantially reduced, we may have to look to other ways to provide sulfur to agricultural soils.

The major plant nutrients, their sources, and some basic information on nutrient deficiency symptoms which can be observed in the garden are displayed in the accompanying table (pp. 34–35).

The micronutrients are a perfect example of the fine tuning of nature. They are absolutely essential in tiny, almost unmeasurable amounts (parts per million), yet in larger quantities they can become harmful and even toxic. Most soils contain ample amounts of the seven trace nutrients, but certain conditions can cause them either to be used up or to become unavailable. Therefore, although you cannot easily supplement your garden's micronutrient supply, it is important to know the proper conditions for making it useful.

*Iron.* Unless iron is present, chlorophyll cannot be created in plant leaves. It is also an important component of certain plant enzymes. Most soils contain sufficient iron for healthy plant growth, but high alkalinity (pH over 7.8) can cause it to become tightly bound to the soil. Adding more iron would not solve the problem; only lowering the pH will. Iron is commonly added to soils with the application of greensand or glauconite.

*Boron.* A crucial and widely used nutrient, boron has at least sixteen different functions in plants, from being essential to flowering and seed germination to assisting in nitrogen metabolism. This is one of the micronutrients that is used up quickly by plants, and a deficiency will be noticeable as a dieback of tender young leaf and bud growth. Boron shortage can also be caused by liming, since it is available to plants only in acid soils (another good reason for maintaining soil pH at 6.0 to 7.0). Oddly, scientists report that boron deficiency, whether caused by liming or plant uptake, is common only in humid climates east of the Mississippi and particularly in the Northeast. Fortunately, in the process of adding other nutrients and organic matter you will also be adding boron, so it will be very rare that a special addition of boron will be needed. The common sources of boron are animal manures, alfalfa green manure, rock lime (in small quantities), and granite dust.

*Manganese.* This element is another key component in the creation of chlorophyll. Plants exhibit manganese deficiency when young leaves are light green but show a network of dark green veins. Although manganese is plentiful in virtually all soils, it can become unavailable in alkaline conditions (above pH 8.5). In very acid conditions so much manganese can be absorbed that it becomes toxic to plants. Proper pH adjustment is the way to solve manganese problems.

*Zinc.* Plants use zinc to produce starches, which are the key to both healthy root and leaf growth. Without it roots grow abnormally and leaves develop a mottled color and white streaking. Zinc-deficient potatoes and squash will often show brown spots on their leaves. Another symptom of zinc deficiency is a noticeable shortening of stems, and plants seem to be miniaturized.

There is usually a great deal of this nutrient in soils, but it becomes less and less available as pH rises above 5.5. This means that in alkaline conditions zinc deficiency is quite frequent. On the other hand, high levels of zinc in soil become toxic when pH drops below 5.5. Once again, a slightly acid soil condition proves best for nutrient availability. If zinc deficiency still exists, continued application of manures or raw rock phosphate will generally solve the problem.

*Molybdenum.* Vitamins and plant proteins are created with the aid of this nutrient. Additionally, plants need molybdenum in order to take in and use nitrates. A deficiency is almost indistinguishable from nitrogen deficiency except in the cabbage family, where it is indicated by narrower than normal leaves. Shortages of molybdenum are rare, but can occur in acid soils.

*Copper.* Copper is highly toxic in more than mi-nute quantities, and it is impossible to add a correct amount of it directly to soil without sophisticated equipment. It is used by plant roots during nitrogen absorption, and a deficiency is difficult to detect, except in onions, where the skins fail to develop their characteristic brown color.

Clay and loam soils generally have adequate copper, but as organic content increases, copper becomes tightly bound to soil. This has led some scientists to expect copper deficiency in highly organic soils, but this has not been confirmed. If you wish to add very small amounts of copper without danger of overdose, wood shavings, sawdust, and grass clippings are recommended sources.

*Chlorine.* Most of us know chlorine as being a highly toxic gas. In the gaseous form it can kill almost any organism, yet when combined with sodium to form sodium chloride, it becomes common table salt. In this form chlorine is essential to life, and plants must have it in order to release oxygen during photosynthesis. A deficiency will produce stubby roots and wilting of plants in conditions when they would normally not wilt. An excess of salt is equally damaging, since high sodium levels are toxic to most plants. Salt is highly water soluble and tends to wash downward in soil. Fortunately, chlorine is added to soil in rainfall, and some plants can absorb it directly from the air, so a deficiency is probably possible only in garden beds and greenhouses which are constantly under glass.

When gardeners who use chemical fertilizers need to add nutrients to the soil, they have a simple procedure to follow. They find out how many pounds per acre of NPK are in the soil and then add the appropriate chemical fertilizer to meet the need. Perhaps this simple process is what leads so many gardeners to the nonorganic method despite the losses in long-term soil texture, humus content, and overall fertility.

For an intensive organic gardener the task of determining how much of a given nutrient to add to soil is more complex but not necessarily more difficult. By using the procedure outlined on page 36 you should be able to add enough (but not too much) of the essential macronutrients along with a little dose of the micronutrients.

MAJOR PLANT NUTRIENTS

| Nutrient | Sources | Deficiency Symptoms | Notes |
|---|---|---|---|
| **Nitrogen** | Rotted animal manure (best if protected from rain) (very good) | Foliage is yellow-green instead of normal dark green. In older plants, yellowing occurs first in older leaves. | Fresh manures are fairly high in nitrogen, but since they are also very high in undecomposed organic matter, when added to the soil, organisms that attack this material may also consume all the nitrogen as well. This is only a temporary problem, because when the decomposition nears completion, the nitrogen is again available for plants. It does mean that fresh manures or fresh organic matter should not be applied just before planting or turned into the soil during the growing season. |
| | Compost (good) | | |
| | Legume green manure crops (good) (see Figure 51) | Size of leaves is reduced. | |
| | Nonlegume green manure crops (good) | Edges of leaves turn yellow or brown. | |
| | Fish meal or emulsion (good) | | |
| | Blood meal (very good, but expensive) | | Sewage sludges may be high in nitrogen, but in some cases are also contaminated with industrial wastes, heavy metals, or other toxic substances. Unless sewage material has been certified free of toxic material *do not use it* in your vegetable garden. |
| | Cottonseed meal (very good) | | |
| | Bone meal (fair) | | |
| | Grass clippings (good if fresh) | | |
| | Fresh animal manure (fair to good, but can cause problems) *see Notes* | | |
| | Leaves (fair to good) | | |
| | Sewage sludge and miscellaneous soil amendments (poor to very good) *see Notes* | | |
| **Phosphorus** | Soft or hard rock phosphate (very good) | Stems turn purple | When pH is less than 4 or over 8.5, phosphorus becomes bound to the soil and cannot be used by plants. |
| | Colloidal phosphate (very good) | Leaf veins turn purple | |
| | Compost (good) | Retarded maturity | Rock and bone meal sources of P contain a large amount of the nutrient, which becomes available to plants over time, though only a small percentage is immediately available. They need not be applied every year. Rock phosphate is usually necessary every three to four years. |
| | Rotted animal manures (good) | Poor yields (especially common in early spring plantings of cabbage family plants) | |
| | Fresh animal manures (fair) | | Bone meal is also alkaline and should not be added to soils where alkalinity is a problem. |
| | Bone meal (very good, but expensive) *see Notes* | | |

## MAJOR PLANT NUTRIENTS (cont.)

| Nutrient | Sources | Deficiency Symptoms | Notes |
|---|---|---|---|
| **Potassium** | Granite dust (very good)<br><br>Compost (fair)<br><br>Greensand (very good)<br><br>Wood ashes (very good)<br><br>Seaweed (good)<br><br>Cottonseed meal (fair)<br><br>Alfalfa green manure (very good)<br><br>Sul-po-mag (a soil amendment) | Lowered resistance to disease<br><br>Low yields<br><br>Mottled, speckled, or curled leaves (especially older leaves) | Potassium is concentrated in the leaves of plants, but is readily leached out by water. If green manures or grass clippings are to be used as a mulch to supply potassium, they must be protected from rain until used.<br><br>Wood ashes must also be protected from rain. They are also alkaline. Be sure not to burn colored newspaper or plastics with your wood if you plan to use it in the garden. Colored inks and plastics contain lead and other toxic substances. |
| **Calcium** | Rock lime or dolomitic limestone (best)<br><br>Wood ashes (good)<br><br>Compost (good)<br><br>Bone meal (good)<br><br>Shells (good) | Deformed terminal leaves, buds, and branches<br><br>Poor plant structure (weak stems, etc.)<br><br>Celery black heart, lettuce tip burn, internal browning of cabbage, cavity spot in carrots, blossom end rot. | Calcium is lost by water leaching downward through the soil.<br><br>Lime can be added by turning it into the top few inches of the soil in the fall. It can also be added with compost or manure, and helps speed up the decomposition process.<br><br>Rock lime should be used rather than hydrated lime. It is less subject to leaching and need be applied only every few years. |
| **Magnesium** | Dolomitic limestone or rock lime (good)<br><br>Rock phosphate (fair)<br><br>Compost (good)<br><br>Manures (good)<br><br>Sul-po-mag (a soil amendment) | Lack of green color in leaves between the veins. Occurs first in older leaves. | Magnesium is generally plentiful except in sandy soils.<br><br>In most cases occasional liming provides all the necessary magnesium.<br><br>Epsom salts can be used as a foliar spray (in low concentrations) to combat Mg deficiency. |
| **Sulfur** | Acid rain (unavoidable in the eastern U.S.)<br><br>Aluminum sulfate (not recommended)<br><br>Sul-po-mag (a soil amendment) | Similar symptoms to nitrogen deficiency, but on younger leaves. | Sulfur is almost never in short supply. |

*(a) Conduct a soil test.* Your results will tell you if you have low, medium, or high levels of usable (soluble) nitrogen, phosphorus, and potassium. These levels are roughly equivalent to the following levels of nutrients:

|  | *high* | *medium* | *low* |
|---|---|---|---|
| Nitrogen | | | |
| | 200 lbs/acre | 125 lbs/acre | 50 lbs/acre |
| | .5 lb/100 sq ft | .3 lb/100 sq ft | .1 lb/100 sq ft |
| Phosphorus | | | |
| | 250 lbs/acre | 175 lbs/acre | 85 lbs/acre |
| | .6 lb/100 sq ft | .4 lb/100 sq ft | .2 lb/100 sq ft |
| Potassium | | | |
| | 200 lbs/acre | 125 lbs/acre | 65 lbs/acre |
| | .5 lb/100 sq ft | .3 lb/100 sq ft | .15 lb/100 sq ft |

*(b) Determine how much NPK you want in each garden bed depending upon what you plan to grow.* Heavy feeders prefer high levels of all three nutrients. (Heavy feeders are plants like cucumbers, tomatoes, melons, eggplant, squash, and most greens.) Light feeders (root crops) prefer medium nitrogen and medium to high phosphorus and potassium. Legumes prefer medium nitrogen and medium to medium high phosphorus and potassium.

*(c) Figure how much of a particular source of nutrients you must add to obtain the desired level.* This is not difficult. First, take the desired level of nutrients, and then subtract from the figures (in lbs/100 sq ft) the amount you already have present (as determined by the soil test). The result will be the amount you must add in fertilizer. Next, consult the chart on NPK percentages in common organic fertilizers. For example, since fresh cow manure has approximately .4 percent nitrogen, it will have .4 lb nitrogen per 100 lbs manure and bedding. If your soil test showed you that your soil has low nitrogen (.1 lb/100 sq ft), and you want high nitrogen (.5 lb/100 sq ft), you will need .4 lb of nitrogen per 100 sq ft of garden space. Since cow manure has .4 lb/100 pounds, you should add 100 lbs of the manure per 100 sq ft of garden space. This same process could be performed for any of the sources of nitrogen, phosphorus, or potassium. Fortunately, you will be adding all three in the same 100 pounds of manure, so your actual manual labor in handling the material will be limited to the manure and any possible supplements you may need if the manure does not contain enough of other desired nutrients.

This process is not exact. The problem comes not in the calculations but in the fact that no two piles of manure or compost contain the same amounts of nutrients. Homegrown organic fertilizers vary considerably in their nutrient content, depending upon how they are stored, what the animals may have been fed, the type of bedding used, or the source of materials used in composting. To solve this problem, if you are concerned that you may not be adding enough of a nutrient or that you are adding too much, conduct a soil test about three weeks after adding the material. If the results are not satisfactory, you can supplement, using commercial organic fertilizers which have a guaranteed analysis.

Some last words of caution. If you err on the side of excess, you will probably not have much of a problem with phosphorus or potassium. On the other hand, excess nitrogen causes many problems and should be avoided.

If you hate doing calculations, you can console yourself in the knowledge that as your soil improves the need for them will diminish. On the other hand, you can always use the "shotgun" method and just hope for the best.

### 3. Building Soil Humus

Soil humus is so valuable to intensive gardening that it is essential to understand its function in promoting healthy plant growth before going into how to build it.

We have already discussed the important role of humus in providing water retention and drainage as well as aeration. But there is an even more important job humus performs known as "cation" exchange. It is a complex process, which is crucial to organic gardening methods, even though most gardeners and farmers know little about it. Without becoming too technical, here is an explanation of how it works.

Every substance is composed of molecules, which are combinations of incredibly small particles called atoms. Atoms themselves are made up of even smaller particles, known as protons, neutrons, and electrons (see Figure 53). These pieces are arranged in a way that resembles a miniature solar system: protons and neutrons combined together to form a nucleus or "sun" and electrons that orbit around the nucleus like "planets." Elec-

## NPK PERCENTAGES IN COMMON ORGANIC MATERIALS

| Manures* | N | P | K |
|---|---|---|---|
| Cow | .4 | .3 | .44 |
| Horse | .65–.76 | .3–.6 | .5–.65 |
| Pig | .3 | .3–.4 | .45 |
| Sheep and goats | .65 | .46 | .23 |
| Chicken | 1.1–1.8 | 1.0 | .5 |
| Turkey | 1.3 | .7 | .5 |
| Rabbit | 2.0 | 1.0 | .5 |
| *Commercially Available Materials* | | | |
| Blood meal | 9.0–15.00 | 1.0–1.3 | .7–1.0 |
| Bone meal (steamed) | 1.0–4.0 | 20.0–30.0 | 0–.2 |
| Bone meal (raw) | 3.0–4.0 | 20.0–24.0 | 0 |
| Cottonseed meal | 6.5–8.0 | 2.0–3.0 | 1.0–2.0 |
| Fish emulsion | 5.0 | 2.4 | 1.2 |
| Fish meal | 8.0–10.5 | 4.0–9.0 | 2.0–3.0 |
| Hoof and horn meal | 7.0–15.0 | 0–2.0 | 0 |
| Kelp meal | 1.0 | 0 | 12.0 |
| Greensand | 0 | 1.5 | 5.0–6.7 |
| Granite dust | 0 | 0 | 3.0–5.0 |
| Hard rock phosphate | 0 | 0 | 25.0–33.0 |
| Soft rock phosphate | 0 | 0 | 15.0–20.0 |
| *Collectible and Grow-Your-Own Materials* | | | |
| Alfalfa green manure | 3.0–4.0 | na | na |
| Alfalfa hay | 1.5–2.5 | .3–.5 | 1.5–2.1 |
| Winter rye green manure | 1.7–2.3 | .18 | 1.05 |
| Seaweed | .5–3.3 | .1–2.0 | 1.0–5.0 |
| Kentucky bluegrass | .66–1.2 | .19–.4 | .71–1.6 |
| Oak leaves | .8 | .35 | .2–.3 |
| Red clover hay | 2.0–3.2 | .25–.5 | 1.28–2.0 |
| Sawdust and wood chips | .2 | .1 | .2 |
| Coffee grounds | 2.1 | .3 | .3 |
| Wood ashes (unleached) | 0 | 1.0–2.0 | 4.0–10.0 |
| Wood ashes (leached) | 0 | 1.0–1.5 | 1.0–3.0 |
| White clover green manure | .5 | .15 | .60 |
| Sewage sludge | .74–6.0 | .33–4.0 | 0–.24 |
| Timothy hay | 1.25 | .55 | 1.0 |
| Cow peas (green forage) | .45–3.0 | .12–.25 | .45–1.45 |
| Oats green manure | 1.3–1.4 | .17 | 1.09 |

\* NPK levels in rotted manures can be slightly higher if kept under cover from rain. If manures are leached, nitrogen and potassium levels will be lower than the values shown.

SOURCES:

JOHN JEAVONS. *How to Grow More Vegetables* (Berkeley, Cal.: Ten Speed Press, 1979).

J. I. RODALE. *Encyclopedia of Organic Gardening* (Emmaus, Pa.: Rodale Press, 1959).

J. I. RODALE. *How to Grow Vegetables & Fruits by the Organic Method* (Emmaus, Pa.: Rodale Press, 1961).

*Sources of Compost* by Fred J. Jisbet in *Country Journal*, July 1979, p. 53.

NOTE:
Compost varies widely in its NPK content, depending upon the materials which are used to produce it. Even so, unless the compost is kept under cover, it will have very little fertilizer value.

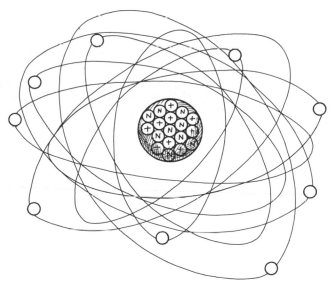

**Figure 53** *An atom contains a positively charged nucleus and orbiting, negatively charged electrons. There are an equal number of protons and neutrons in the nucleus, and the number of electrons orbiting around the nucleus is equal to the number of protons.*

trons are negatively charged (−) and the nucleus is positively charged (+). (Neutrons have a neutral charge or no charge.) Since opposites attract, electrons are normally kept in their orbits around the nucleus (each atom has an equal number of protons and electrons so as to keep this balance). However, when atoms combine together to form molecules, quite often an electron "escapes" or is removed for use elsewhere by other molecules. This results in a molecule or "ion" with a missing negative charge, so that its net charge is positive (see Figure 54). The molecule that captures the

**Figure 54** *An example of an ion with a positive charge, a cation. When the atoms of nitrogen (N) and hydrogen (H) combined to form a molecule of $NH_4$, one electron was set "free" leaving a net positive charge.*

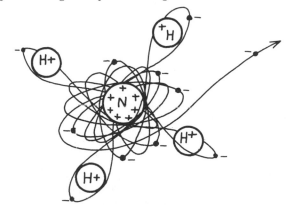

*Nitrogen has seven of its own electrons.*
*Hydrogen have one each.*
*$NH_4$ has ten and one is set free.*

extra electron has then a net negative charge. The positive molecules are called "cations" and the negative molecules "anions." Since they are of opposite charges, the ions themselves are often attracted to each other.

This becomes important when we discover that some of the important nutrients used by plants are found as ions in the soil. Both cations and anions are found in the soil, but for some reason soil particles themselves are negatively charged, and only the cations are attracted to the soil. These cations seek to attach themselves to the soil particles. Their ability to do this is determined by the number of attachment "sites" that a particle has. The more surface area a particle has, the more cation sites it has (see Figure 55).

Now comes the crucial action. Plant roots and

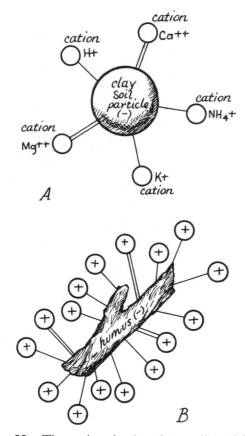

**Figure 55** *The number of cations that a soil particle can "hold" is a factor of its surface area; a particle of clay holding on to a number of positively charged cations is shown in A; a particle of humus, even though its actual size may be no larger, has more surface area, and thus more cation receptor sites, as shown in B.*

rootlets weave their way through the soil in search of nutrients, many of which are found as cations. When a rootlet comes near a particle of soil that is holding a number of desired cations, the plant gives off a hydrogen ion with a positive charge ($H^+$). $H^+$ ions always take priority over all other cations in electrical attraction, and so the $H^+$ ions "bump" loose the nutrient cations and take their place on the soil particles. The nutrient cations are then absorbed by the plant roots and taken upward for use in growth and photosynthesis (see Figure 56).

Nutrients that are absorbed in this way are ammonium ($NH_4^+$), potassium ($K^+$), calcium ($Ca^{++}$), magnesium ($Mg^+$), and most micronutrients.

Other nutrients are not found as cations and do not attach themselves to soil particles the same way. These nutrients are usually negatively charged (anions) and are absorbed by plant roots when the roots take in water (see Figure 57). Both nitrates ($NO_3^-$) and phosphates are water soluble anions and are absorbed in this way. (Phosphates, however, have the ability to bind themselves to the soil, while nitrates do not.) Anions, like nitrates, are dependent upon water for their movement in the soil and because of this can be easily washed downward out of the reach of plant roots by rainwater. This fact in itself is one of the major reasons why chemical nitrates are such a water pollution problem in the United States. Chemical fertilizers are very high in soluble nitrates, in fact so high that not all of them can be absorbed by plant roots before they are washed downward in the soil. The nitrates then find their way into the underground water table and then into streams and lakes. Once in surface waters, the nutrient becomes food for another plant, algae, which eventually clogs the water and dies from overpopulation. This is called eutrophication and is one of the most serious and widespread forms of water pollution.

What does all this have to do with humus? Humus is important to all this because it is the most effective holder of nutrients in the soil. Humus particles are very porous; they have lots of surface area, which means they have plenty of sites for cations to attach to. Humus is even more effective than soil particles at providing cation exchange sites. This means that a humus-rich soil is

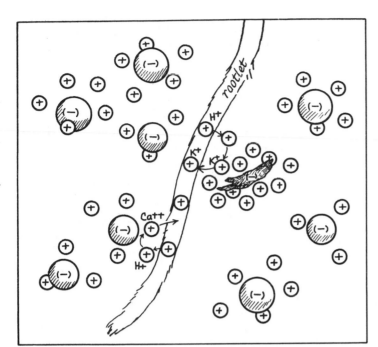

**Figure 56** *Rootlets in the soil are surrounded by soil particles which hold cations. When the plant needs a nutrient cation, it releases an H+ ion, which "bumps" a cation off of a soil particle so that it can be absorbed by the plant.*

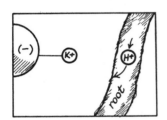

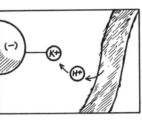

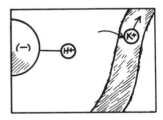

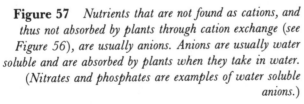

1. $H^+$ ion in the root is moving downward and toward the soil.

2. $H^+$ is released by the root.

3. $K^+$ ion is bumped by the $H^+$ ion.

4. $K^+$ ion is absorbed by the root for use by the plant.

**Figure 57** *Nutrients that are not found as cations, and thus not absorbed by plants through cation exchange (see Figure 56), are usually anions. Anions are usually water soluble and are absorbed by plants when they take in water. (Nitrates and phosphates are examples of water soluble anions.)*

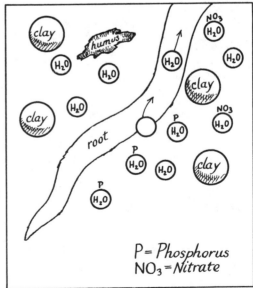

$P$ = Phosphorus
$NO_3$ = Nitrate

capable of providing considerably better cation exchange than almost any mineral soil (see Figures 58–60).

Humus also acts like a sponge to hold gravitational and capillary water. Since anion nutrients are soluble and are absorbed by plants in water, humus acts to prevent loss of these nutrients through leaching or erosion.

Finally, we should recall that many of the nutrients in the soil being held for use by plants came from the humus-building process in the first place. Humus is certainly a versatile performer. It supplies the nutrients, prepares them for use, and serves them to plants in the needed amounts at a gradual rate. What more could we ask for?

Most of today's agricultural soils are deficient in humus and have less than a 5 percent humus content, although a well-managed farm or garden soil can have as much as 10 percent humus. Organic farming and gardening associations most often establish that for proper organic growing conditions a 5 percent humus content is the minimum. But, as with nutrients, more is not always better. Muck soils formed in swampy areas build up a humus content of 10 to 40 percent, and peat bogs range from 40 percent to 100 percent humus. In both of these cases drainage is poor, most nutrients are used up quickly or leached out, and soil microbial activity is low. If these wet soils can be drained and

loosened, they can often be very productive, but without a rich soil flora and fauna they are almost useless as an agricultural resource. This illustrates an important point about humus. Although humus alone is an important measure of soil fertility it is only valuable where conditions are dynamic and where there are also adequate nutrients.

Humus is by nature a rich dark color. If you have a soil that has this dark chocolate coloration, you probably have a good humus content. The exception is in soils with excess manganese, which take on a dark color even if humus is not present. Of course humus-rich soils also have a spongelike texture which distinguishes them immediately from manganese soils.

In your soil-building program you should use the following rules of thumb:

1. Keep soil humus content above 5 percent. This can be accurately determined only by a soil test, which you can do yourself with one of the more expensive test kits, or by sending a soil sample to a reliable testing lab. If you are working to improve humus content by using regular additions of organic material, it will be necessary only to have this test made once every few years to check your progress. If you are confident that you already have a humus-rich soil or that your soil-building program is making steady progress, the humus test is probably not essential.

**Figure 58** *Composting organic material before adding it to soil breaks down most substances into humus. Garden of Eric Laser and Peggy Smith in Maine.*

**Figure 59** *Compost piles in the Finger Lakes region of New York.*

2. Provide a constant supply of fresh humus. The action of soil organisms both produces and destroys soil humus. Any biologically active soil must have regular infusions of new humus to replace what is lost to this microbial action as well as from erosion by wind and rain.

3. Always add well-decomposed organic matter. Any addition of organic matter into soil produces an increase of microbial activity. This increase is generally desirable because its ultimate result is the release of nutrients into the soil. But the more fresh (undecomposed) material you add, the greater the risk you face that all that soil life will increase too much and consume large quantities of humus as well. Add to this risk the fact that microbial activity increases with soil temperature, and we find that in some warm climates (and perhaps in warm microclimates like covered beds and under cloches) the addition of fresh organic matter will spur so much soil activity that the result can be a net decrease in humus. This is exemplified by the soil structure of tropical regions. Temperatures are so warm that soil activity remains high all year. This produces a condition where any organic matter that falls to the ground is rapidly decomposed and its nutrients recycled into plants. What little humus is left is also quickly decomposed. As a result, tropical soils tend to be very low in humus content and have very shallow topsoils. The lush natural vegetation of the tropics is well suited to this condition, but whenever these soils have been used for agriculture, they are rapidly depleted and quickly become infertile.

Obviously it is not always possible to add only composted or well-rotted material to your beds. However, the use of fresh material should be kept to a minimum, especially in beds that are under lights or cloches, where soil life activity is especially high. The best practice is to add organic matter in the form of rotted manure (two months minimum in

PHOTO BY TIMOTHY FISHER.

**Figure 61** *At the end of the summer growing season this hay mulch can be turned into the soil to add to its humus content.*

warm climates, three to four months minimum in cooler climates like the Northeast), compost, decomposed leaves, or various hays that have been allowed to spoil for a year or longer (see Figure 61).

4. Don't depend upon green manures to improve humus content in a short time. Many people have erroneously assumed that constant use of green manures will rapidly improve soil texture and humus content. This is not necessarily true.

Green manures have benefits in providing and conserving nutrients. Winter cover crops will capture soil nutrients and hold them over the winter, preventing them from being leached away by melting snow or spring rains. Leguminous green manures can obtain large quantities of nitrogen from the air, and, when turned under, provide this nutrient for use by following crops. But there is considerable question about the efficacy of green manure crops for adding to humus content. Some experts believe that the increased biological activity caused by adding green organic matter to soil results in a possible net loss of humus under certain conditions (particularly heat and high humidity).

PHOTO BY TIMOTHY FISHER.

**Figure 60** *Compost piles at the Coolidge Center for the Advancement of Agriculture in Massachusetts.*

41

From our own experience we believe that green manures have a role to play in helping to build soil humus if they are used in combination with the addition of other organic matter and if they are used in the spring and fall when temperatures are lower. This means that although the green manure crop can be planted or grown at any time you choose, the best time to turn the crop into the soil is either in the early spring or fall. Our own unscientific testing seems to indicate that there is no appreciable difference in humus content of soils between beds that received both green manure and compost and those that received only compost. On the other hand, beds that received only green manure had a noticeably poorer texture after two years compared with those that received compost. Nutrient levels in all the beds were comparable, yet production in the composted beds appeared to be better. The added benefit of the green manure was in eliminating the need to add as much fertilizer, not in quickly improved soil texture.

Of course, if you have more patience than we do and are willing to wait a few years before the humus levels of your soil build up, you can rely more heavily upon green manures. If used in the right way many gardeners have indicated that they can slowly improve humus content using only winter cover crops and a rotation of leguminous green manures.

5. Once you have reached a satisfactory humus level, you can reduce your organic matter additions. While building organic matter in our soils we have regularly added 3 to 6 inches of rotted manure or compost to each bed every year. In beds covered by solar intensive devices we have added slightly more, but in regular applications between crops. However, once our beds become established, we have found that cutting back to 1 to 2 inches of organic material is sufficient to maintain quality in summer beds, and 2 to 4 inches is sufficient in glazed beds. In calculating this figure we have included turning under spoiled and decomposed mulches.

Lastly, if you subscribe to the "no-till" method of gardening, we suspect you will find our method extremely labor intensive. There is no doubt that the most laborious part of intensive gardening is soil building. It certainly was for the early French intensive gardeners, who had not only to mix the soil by hand but also to carry the manure on their backs! But we believe that the results are worth the effort. After building a good soil, you will want to go back to the no-till/heavy mulch method. We describe in Chapter 4 the no-till methods used by some of the gardeners we visited while preparing this book.

### 4. Balancing pH

Potential hydrogen or pH, discussed earlier in this chapter, is a measure of the existence of $H^+$ ions in the soil. Since in any soil $H^+$ ions take top priority for cation attachment sites, an excess of $H^+$ ions results in fewer spaces for nutrient cations to attach themselves. This condition is commonly referred to as "acid." On the other hand, if there is an excess of $OH^-$ ions (hydroxyl ions) in the soil, it produces what is known as an alkaline condition. In alkaline soils, $OH^-$ ions combine with whatever cations are available (usually nutrients), taking them away from exchange sites and locking them up.

This means that in either an acid or alkaline soil nutrients become unavailable to plant roots. In acid soils they are being bumped out of exchange sites by the abundance of $H^+$ ions, and in alkaline soils they are being "stolen" by $OH^-$ ions. Obviously the way to solve this problem is to have a balanced amount of each or a neutral soil where neither of these ions gains control.

As indicated earlier, the desirable pH level for most plants is 6.5 to 7.0 (see Figure 62). There are exceptions, and they fall mostly into the category of acid-loving plants like strawberries, blueberries, and potatoes. Some plants, like beets, seem to prefer a slightly alkaline soil, pH 7.0–8.0. A quick check of the pH chart that comes with most soil test kits or in any basic gardening book can give you specifics on individual plant species.

You should be especially careful always to have proper soil pH. If your soil varies considerably from the neutral point, you can have some serious problems. Aluminum becomes available as a cation as soil pH rises above 8.0 and becomes toxic at levels not much higher. Aluminum is normally found in all soils, but is usually bound tightly to soils particles and cannot be taken up by plant roots. The cation form, however, is taken up by plants.

At very low pH (below 5) not only are most macronutrients less available, but some trace nutrients (iron and manganese in particular) become too available and can cause imbalances in plant metabolism (see Figure 62).

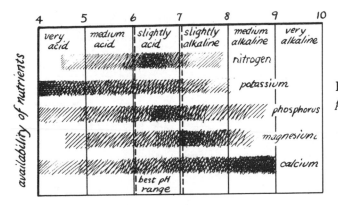

**Figure 62** *The availability of nutrients for use by plants is a factor of the pH level of the soil.*

Many gardeners feel they can determine the soil pH by looking around to see which weeds are most common in their garden. Weeds are often a good indicator of pH levels because each species has a specific pH preference. On the other hand, we have seen situations where weeds are very inaccurate indicators of pH because of other complex soil conditions. This being the case, it is wise to keep the soil test kit handy and use it regularly to test for soil pH. We usually test once in the spring, before adding fertilizer or other organic matter, then again shortly before planting. Adjustments can be made easily at these times, but they are more difficult once crops are established. We test again in the fall before planting our winter vegetables or cover crops.[1]

Frequent addition of well-decomposed organic matter has what is known as a "buffering" effect upon soil pH. A buffered soil tends to stay at a stable pH, because the constant decomposition of organic matter releases both acidic and alkaline compounds in roughly equal amounts. This means that as your soil texture and humus content improve, it becomes less and less common that pH adjustments are necessary—pH will tend to stabilize at around 6.5 to 7.0. Of course, if you are adding a very acidic organic substance like pine needles or peat moss, this buffering effect can be negated.

You can use the following rules to guide your efforts in balancing pH:

1. If acidity is your problem (as in most of the eastern U.S.), you must add an alkaline substance to the

[1]For more information about weeds, consult "Weeds as Indicators of Soil Conditions" by Dr. Stuart Hill, McDonald College, McGill University, Montreal, Quebec.

soil. There are a few to choose from: rock lime; wood ashes (unleached); bone meal.

Rock lime is the most commonly used pH conditioner. The amount you use depends upon the size of the particles in your soil. Clay soils are more difficult to adjust because there are more particles and thus more places for $H^+$ ions to "hide." The following amounts of ground dolomitic limestone are recommended:

| | |
|---|---|
| Light sandy soil | 5 lbs/100 sq ft will raise pH one point |
| Sandy loam | 7 lbs/100 sq ft will raise pH one point |
| Good humus-rich loam | 10 lbs/100 sq ft will raise pH one point |
| Heavy clay | 12–15 lbs/100 sq ft will raise pH one point |

One application of ground limestone is usually effective for two to four years. Be conservative in your use of limestone, as it is far easier to adjust an acid soil than to correct an alkaline soil that has received an excess of lime.

Wood ashes (from hardwoods) are also an alkaline substance containing significant amounts of calcium and potassium. Rain will quickly leach out these minerals, so keep your ashes under cover. There are no good rules for rate of application of wood ashes, but since they are much more soluble than ground lime, it is wise to apply less than you would of lime. They are also not as long lasting in the soil and may need to be reapplied every year. It is very important to use only ashes from hardwood and not ashes from burned trash or newspaper with colored ink. Trash and colored ink contain heavy metals harmful to human beings, if not plants. These metals generally do not burn or go up in smoke. If you do not produce your own ashes, be sure to inquire about the source of your supply before mixing any in your soil.

2. If your soil is alkaline, the traditional solution has been to add sulfur. Sulfur mixes with hydrogen and oxygen to form sulfuric acid, and this lowers pH. Unfortunately, most sulfur for pH adjustment is provided using calcium sulfate (gypsum), which adds more calcium to soils tending to have more than enough calcium already. Another traditional solution has been to add borax, but excess boron can easily kill many plants. Ammonium sulfate is another chemical used by nonorganic growers.

The preferable way to reduce alkalinity is through the addition of acidic organic matter. Cottonseed meal, acid peat moss, or decomposed oak leaves will all gradually reduce pH to acceptable levels. Pine needles can be used for some crops like strawberries or blueberries, but many vegetables find the tannins and acids of pine needles to be toxic.

Humic acids in compost and other acids found in fresh animal manures tend to neutralize pH as well. Fifty pounds of manure (with minimal bedding), or 2 cubic feet spread over 100 square feet of loose loamy soil will generally lower pH one point.

## CONCLUSION

There is little doubt that the best soils produce the best vegetables. The advantages of building a good, humus-rich, nutritionally balanced soil are the obvious positive effects it will have in producing larger yields, earlier crops, and less work for you. But there are some additional benefits often hidden to the eye.

Scientific research is beginning to confirm that plants grown in healthy organic soils have more nutritional value than their counterparts grown in chemically boosted mineral soils. Evidently the balance of trace minerals and the more even growth cycle are capable of producing crops with small, but measurably increased levels of vitamins and minerals necessary in the human diet.

Additionally, recent attention to biological pest control methods has looked into the role that certain plant hormones have upon insect pests. It now appears that under stressful conditions of drought, nutrient deficiency, or poor soil texture, plants either fail to produce some insect-repelling hormones or instead produce excesses of other hormones that attract some pests. This may explain the observation of many organic gardeners that pests somehow seem to prefer the least healthy of plants, leaving the robust individuals alone or less ravaged. In the rich organic soils of the intensive garden stressful conditions are largely eliminated by proper soil management. Our own experience confirms this notion. As our soil has improved over the years, our pest problems have become noticeably less severe, and some pests that rampage through the neighbors' gardens are endangered species in ours.

This soil building is hard work. Of all the activities in intensive gardening it is the most trying of physical stamina. But it is also invigorating and healthful for the soil and the gardener.

FURTHER READINGS:

ALTHER, R., and R. RAYMOND. *Improving Garden Soil with Green Manures* (Charlotte, Vt.: Garden Way, 1974). *A short booklet with practical suggestions.*

BUCKMAN, H. O., and N. C. BRADY. *The Nature and Properties of Soils* (New York: Macmillan, 1969). *A widely used college textbook on agricultural soils.*

CAMPBELL, STU. *Let It Rot!* (Charlotte, Vt.: Garden Way, 1975). *A how-to book on home composting.*

FARB, PETER. *Living Earth* (New York: Harper Colophon, 1959). *A readable look at soil biology.*

FORTH, H. D., and L. M. TURK. *Fundamentals of Soil Science* (New York: Wiley, 1972). *A basic textbook.*

GOLUEKE, CLARENCE. *Composting: A Study of the Process and Its Principles* (Emmaus, Pa.: Rodale, 1972). *For advanced readers.*

HOWARD, SIR ALBERT. *The Soil and Health* (New York: Schocken, 1972). *A worldwide view of the importance of soil health and humus to agriculture, by a major pioneer in organic methods.*

HYAMS, EDWARD. *Soil and Civilization* (New York: Harper Colophon, 1952, 1976). *A history of the relationship between human civilizations and their use and abuse of the soil.*

JANICK, J., R. SCHERY, F. WOODS, and V. RUTTAN. *Plant Science: An Introduction to World Crops* (San Francisco: W. H. Freeman and Co., 1974). *Contains a very good chapter on soil science and its relation to plant growth and health.*

KOEPF, H. H. *Compost: What It Is, How It Is Made, What It Does* (Biodynamic Farming and Gardening Association, 1966).

LOGSDON, GENE. *Gardener's Guide to Better Soil* (Emmaus, Pa.: Rodale, 1975).

*Organic Fertilizers: Which Ones and How to Use Them.* The Staff of *Organic Gardening* magazine (Emmaus, Pa.: Rodale, 1973). *Provides good information on a wide variety of fertilizers and their application.*

*Soil.* U. S. Department of Agriculture, Yearbook of Agriculture, 1957.

# 3

# PLANNING AN INTENSIVE GARDEN

Timothy Fisher and Kathleen Kolb

ANY GARDENER will find it worthwhile to plan his garden, for a little attention given beforehand to location, soil, and varieties of vegetables to grow can save work and make the garden more enjoyable and productive. Planning is perhaps even more important in an intensive garden, where maximum production in a limited area relies on efficient coordination of the various aspects involved.

Intensive gardening methods seek to use the full growing season and the entire area available. This does not imply that a longer season or larger area are more appropriate for intensive methods, but only that these two factors, time and space, reach their fullest potential in the intensive garden. The gardener also plans to use water, fertilizer, light, and labor as economically as he can.

This takes a lot of coordination, but becomes easier with practice. You will find that after a couple of seasons the different elements of the intensive garden, along with the other requirements of vegetable growing, will be sufficiently embedded in your consciousness for you to be able to manage it easily, with successively better results. Initially, though, a plan is enormously helpful.

## CHOOSING A LOCATION

Your first decision is where to put the garden. If you have only one possibility, it will be an easy decision, but if you have a choice, there is a lot to consider. Location is determined on the basis of soil, microclimate, and accessibility. You will also have to consider how your vegetable garden fits in with the other ways in which you use your property. Few locations will afford all the desired ingredients, but an awareness of them at least permits you to make selective compromises.

Soil is a basic criterion of location. The soil chapter in this book will help you identify the best garden soils as well as modify existing soils. You will be able to alter almost any soil situation enough to create a successful intensive garden, but if you have a choice, naturally choose the best. A soil test is very valuable for showing you the weak and strong points of your soil so that you will know what you do and don't need to add to it.

In urban areas and near highways the soil should also be tested for lead contamination from car exhaust and industrial pollutants. A vegetable garden should be at least 50 feet from a busy street

45

and shielded from the road by a hedge or fence to lessen the effect of exhaust. There is also a danger that there may be lead in the soil where a lead-painted building once stood. Leafy vegetables, particularly, absorb lead from the air and soil, so a concern about lead poisoning may prove critical to your garden location.

Much of the work you do with your soil will consist of adding organic matter to it. Locating or making and storing these materials should be a part of your overall garden plan and schedule. A space may need to be provided for making compost. Leaves, which are useful in the garden all year, must be gathered in the fall and stored or composted. Manure is available all year, but in the spring you may be competing for it with your fellow gardeners, so a stored supply would be convenient.

The ability of soil to hold or drain water can make it a desirable or undesirable garden spot. A loam is generally considered ideal (see Chapter 2). It neither drains too quickly (like sand) nor refuses to absorb water at all (like clay). Either extreme could result in drought or flood. The selection of a site that is slightly above the surrounding ground level, perhaps on a slight slope, gives you lower ground for excess water to drain off to (see Figure 63).

Land with a slope is subject to potential erosion, particularly when tilling leaves its soil exposed to the weather. It is quite possible that this land has lost much of its topsoil before you ever garden it, and you will have to give it special treatment if you garden there. Though a slight slope to your garden site is often beneficial in terms of water and frost drainage, a slope of any severity requires you to take adequate measures to prevent erosion. (Suggestions for how to do this will be found in Chapter 4.)

## MICROCLIMATE

Another factor in determining the location of your garden is the microclimate. We are all aware of climatic differences between different areas of the country and of the climatic zones shown on USDA maps. However, your garden site is part of a smaller zone that may or may not answer to the generalized description of the large zone you are in on the map. This pocket, or microclimate, may be significantly warmer or colder, wetter or drier, than surrounding areas. This is due to solar and wind exposure, water and air drainage, elevation, topography, and other more subtle considerations.

As oceans modify the larger climate, smaller

**Figure 63**  *A garden site slightly above surrounding ground level will aid in water and frost drainage. Garden of Sam and Elizabeth Smith in Massachusetts.*

bodies of water are modifiers of the microclimate. This is noticeable in the Finger Lakes region of New York State, where vineyards thrive on the hillsides that form the lake valley. Once you crest the hill and leave the valley, you enter a colder region no longer suited to grapes.

Living in the Northern Hemisphere, with the sun always to our south, a garden on a gradual south-facing slope is the ideal exposure. The sun will warm up this area earliest in the spring, and it will receive the longest periods of sunlight during the day. A southern slope also affords protection from the cold northwest winds.

We visited a southern New Hampshire garden on the south slope of a mountain. In many ways it was an unlikely garden site, consisting of little soil and lots of rocks. But dealing with only the relatively small area necessary for an intensive garden, its gardeners were able to add large quantities of organic matter to build a soil. They were more than compensated for their work by a microclimate they estimate to be comparable, because of their southern exposure and cold air drainage, to the general climate fifty miles to their south.

Even if you haven't ideal solar exposure, try at least to stay out of the shade. Trees can be cut down or pruned to allow more sunlight to reach the garden. In addition to shading the garden, tree roots are competing with the vegetables for moisture and soil nutrients. Some tree roots even emit toxins. However, as the photo of vegetables in a Cape Cod peach orchard shows (see Figure 64), an intercropping of trees and vegetables can be successfully managed.

**Figure 65**  *If your garden location is hemmed in by buildings, you can place the garden on the north side of the lot to give it maximum southern exposure. This garden benefits from wind protection and heat storage provided by the wall it's backed against. Garden of Ray Wolf in Pennsylvania.*

If your lot is hemmed in by buildings, put your garden on the north side of the lot to give it maximum southern exposure (see Figure 65). An exception to this rule is that during midsummer cool crops such as spinach and lettuce may prefer areas on the south side of the lot or under trees. If sunlight is unavailable elsewhere, you can still build window boxes or create a garden in a container on a porch or rooftop.

**Figure 64**  *Intercropping trees or vines and vegetables can be successfully managed, as in this Cape Cod peach orchard.*

Wind protection is significant in creating a milder microclimate more conducive to plant growth. The natural topography, a forest, a planted windbreak, hedges, fences, walls, and buildings all serve to modify the force of the wind. The windbreak both raises the temperature and protects plants from breakage caused by strong winds. A windbreak will cause snow to settle behind it, adding moisture to the garden, but it may mean you won't get into the garden as early in the spring. Windbreaks also slow down hot, drying summer winds. Bees don't like strong winds and will pollinate plants sheltered by a windbreak.

Providing shelter from the wind is a feasible site modification in any location. A windbreak may also serve as an erosion control if laid out across a hillside. In a small yard there is a possible problem of the windbreak shading the garden. The roots of a living windbreak could compete with the garden for soil nutrients. There is also a potential competition for a limited garden space, though it would be hard to begrudge space to a living windbreak that consists of fruits, berries, and flowers. Such a windbreak can also attract and provide a habitat for birds and predatory insects that are a major control to destructive insects in the garden. (The windbreak, of course, can also harbor garden pests.) Though generally it takes a period of time to establish an effective living windbreak, a thick planting of tall annual flowers can be grown in one season, and a multiflora rose hedge becomes established in a few years (see Figure 66). Multiflora roses can, however, become pernicious weeds in a milder climate. In Ohio, where author

PHOTO BY TIMOTHY FISHER.

**Figure 67** *In cities, the microclimate is usually warmer than the surrounding countryside due to the wind protection of buildings and the concrete and paving which acts as a thermal mass. Garden of Shui-Ying Lam in Boston, Massachusetts.*

**Figure 66** *A multiflora rose hedge becomes established in a few years. Garden of Ray and Linda Nelson in Maine.*

PHOTO BY TIMOTHY FISHER.

Doscher once lived, birds would spread the seeds everywhere, and the bushes popped up wherever the grass wasn't mowed regularly. Other possible windbreak shrubs are autumn olive, barberry, honeysuckle, euonymous, yew, and arborvitae. All these can also help attract birds to the garden.

A wooden fence provides a quick and effective windbreak. A stone or masonry wall is the most time-consuming and expensive to build. Traditionally, the south side of a masonry wall is the area planned for the earliest crops. In addition to the warmer temperature afforded by the wind protection, the thermal mass of the masonry is warmed during the day by the sun, and this heat is gradually released during the night, creating a favorable microclimate. This is dramatically illustrated in cities, which usually have a warmer microclimate than the surrounding countryside because of the wind protection of the buildings and the enormous amounts of concrete and pavement acting as thermal mass (see Figure 67). Heat

**Figure 68** *Shui-Ying Lam in her urban garden (Boston, Massachusetts).*

also emanates from the concentrated burning of fossil fuels for heating, manufacturing, and transportation.

Despite the preceding advice, an ideal exposure is not essential. Our own garden, located on a northwest slope subject to very strong winds, is very productive even in the short season of northeastern Vermont (see Figure 69). As further compensation, we are afforded the advantage of an orchard location where the trees generally don't bud until after danger of the last frost, not to mention the view.

Cold-air drainage was dramatically illustrated to us in 1979 when our hillside garden enjoyed a four-month frost-free season, while valley gardens in the same town had a period of only forty days between frosts. The farther north you live, the more critical becomes your concern about frosts. A

**Figure 69** *Despite an exposed location on a northwest slope, the hillside allows for a comparatively long growing season due to good frost drainage. Garden of Timothy and Kathleen Fisher in Vermont.*

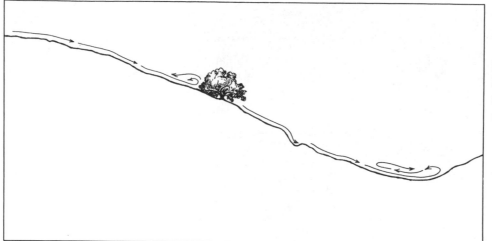

**Figure 70** *Frost drainage on a hillside. Cold air collects behind barriers and in ditches and low areas.*

basic principle to bear in mind is that cold air sinks and hot air rises. Cold air behaves like a fluid, flowing from higher elevations and becoming trapped in low areas, where it can freeze a garden (see Figure 70). A small difference in elevation can make a big difference in the length of your growing season.

Apart from the use of solar intensive devices and covering the garden with sheets, plastic, or blankets, etc., on cold nights, if your summer garden is in a frost pocket, you have a problem. There are, however, a few things you can do to lessen the problem. The first thing to make sure of is that you are allowing as much air flow as possible to lower areas. Remembering that air moves much like water, you can prevent it from flowing to lower ground by a dense forest growth or hedge, a raised road or railway embankment, or a wall, all of which can act like a dam. Try to provide a break in this "dam" to allow the cold air to flow past your garden. Similarly, a garden situated directly below such a "break" in the frost "dam" will be subjected to more frost damage than a garden located just fifty feet to either side of the break.

In mild frost situations even the height of a raised bed can be significant elevation difference to avoid frost damage. One year we had potatoes planted directly in the ground only two feet from an eight-inch raised bed of potatoes. The potatoes in the bed were unaffected by a frost that settled at ground level, killing the potato plants there. In certain situations that raised-bed advantage could be exploited with much higher beds or by building a miniplateau area for the whole garden. On cold

mornings one often notices that frost has settled in drainage ditches and stream beds. This situation could be duplicated in your garden by digging ditches specifically for the cold air to drain into or channel it to lower ground.

## ACCESSIBILITY

Aside from considering soil and microclimate in your choice of a garden location, you should think about access. Whether by truck, tractor, trailer, or car (or boat?), you will want to deliver loads of fertilizer, mulch, and compost material, stakes, cold frames and other needed materials, directly to the garden with a minimum of hand moving. Being able to get to the garden easily yourself is also a consideration, whether you are growing a little salad for summer use or supplying a large vegetable stand as well as your own kitchen. Generally, the closer your garden is to the house the better (see Figure 71). This makes it convenient to go out and pick a few things for a meal or to work in it for short periods of time. On a frosty night it will be easier to run out and cover tender plants. You will be able to keep an eye on it, watching for marauding animals or vandals, and the mere proximity of the garden to the house will discourage some wild animals.

Even in regions with reliable rainfall most gardens will benefit from watering during the dry periods and when seedlings are set out, so your location should include access to water.

Understandably, all the criteria of an ideal garden site rarely concur in one place. You will know which considerations are most important to you

50

PHOTO BY TIMOTHY FISHER.

**Figure 71** *It is convenient for the garden to be close to the house so you can easily work for short periods, pick a few things for a meal, or cover plants on a frosty night. Garden of Heather and Don Parker in Maine.*

and probably add a few of your own. You may be left with a site that seems far short of ideal. Don't let this deter you. The initial labor may be considerable, but the productivity of the garden will be commensurate with the work invested. Perhaps, too, you are a person who is challenged by a difficult spot to make it a place of beauty and usefulness. If so, you will enjoy the satisfaction of terracing, soil building, hedge planting, and fence making.

## LAYOUT

Planning is very helpful in the layout of an intensive garden as well as in deciding where to locate it. In some ways it is nearly architectural, for, unlike field gardening, intensive beds are usually permanent and may make you sorry if they aren't well planned.

Growing beds in the garden can be made modular—of uniform shape—to fit with solar intensive devices and to allow for their interchangeability (see Figure 72). In this case the size of the beds will be determined by the sizes of devices you plan to use, which can either be bought or homemade. The size of these appliances will be affected by the standard dimensions of materials used in their construction.

Beds can also be made in free-form shapes for aesthetic purposes. You may choose to make a few modular and a few free-style beds, depending on how you hope to use the garden. We saw a beautiful intensively gardened yard in Chelsea, Vermont, where vegetables, dye plants, herbs, and flowers were all grown together, bearing more resemblance to flower garden beds than to anything

**Figure 72** *Modular shaped beds allow for the interchangeability of solar intensive devices.*

PHOTO BY PAUL DOSCHER.

**Figure 73**    *An example of free-form beds in Chelsea, Vermont.*

step into a bed, damaging plants and compacting soil. Most people find a bed width of 3 to 5 feet to be comfortable. Some gardeners plan the width of the beds so that they can be straddled with a truck or other vehicle for easy unloading of organic matter (see Figure 74). You may also choose to build the beds narrow enough to be able to straddle them yourself while weeding, digging, or cultivating (see Figure 75). Other people plan the size of their beds so that they will be 100 square feet in area, or a multiple thereof. This can be useful because recommended doses of soil amendments are usually measured per 100 square feet, thus a four-foot-wide bed would be 25 feet long or a five-foot-wide bed 20 feet long. This helps the gardener who wishes to keep accurate records, and gives him/her a unit of comparison. Beds should be short enough to assure that cross traffic won't be difficult. Sometimes a shorter bed is psychologically more satisfying than a longer bed, for the gardener can then tend the whole bed in a short time rather than achieve only part of the job on the long bed. If you are planning beds boxed in with lumber, to conserve lumber bear in mind that standard length lumber comes in multiples of 2 feet.

else (see Figure 73). Though most of the plants were useful or edible, they were arranged for beauty, making a lovely curving border to the lawn. Another intensive garden in the same area had vegetable beds of all shapes and sizes, made that way strictly for the gardeners' enjoyment and delight, creating an unusual swirling mosaic.

The size of the beds will also be determined by other factors. Can you reach all parts of the bed from surrounding paths? This is important, for it is contrary to intensive gardening principles to

Make your paths wide enough to accommodate any carts, wheelbarrows, rototillers, or lawnmowers you will use in the garden. Generally we favor paths at least two feet wide for ease in walk-

**Figure 74**    *The width of garden beds can be planned so they can be straddled by a truck for easy unloading.*

**Figure 75**    *Garden beds can be narrow enough to be straddled while digging, weeding, or cultivating.*

sun to fall on all the plants with minimal shading, as the sun moves across the sky from east to west. In any garden place the tallest plants to the north end of the garden to prevent their shading the other plants. The exception, of course, is where you desire to shade certain plants. Beds can also be arranged in a pattern for their aesthetic appeal.

In deciding how to lay out your garden beds you may want to put solar intensive beds in the part of the garden closest to the house. When you go out to harvest from these beds in below freezing or snowy weather, this may make the trip easier for both you and the produce.

In laying out your garden, space should be provided for whatever compost piles, manure, or mulch storage you expect to need. These may fit right in with the growing beds, or may occupy odd corners left by charting your beds according to the

**Figure 77** *Trellises are another way to economize on garden space. Garden at the Rodale New Farm in Pennsylvania.*

**Figure 76** *By late summer many plants will have become so large that foliage overflows into pathways, making them effectively narrower. Garden of Eric Laser and Peggy Smith in Maine.*

ing through and tending the plants. By late summer many plants will have become so large that foliage overflows into pathways, making them effectively narrower (see Figure 76). However, if land is at a premium, paths can be much narrower (see Figure 77). Some gardeners opt for paths 12 inches to 18 inches wide between beds, which join into wider paths that may be 3 or 4 feet wide. This conserves mulch on the narrow paths if you plan to mulch them, and also saves space. Some traditional French market gardeners had paths only 9 inches wide. In addition to being a spatial economy, narrower paths required far less manure, which the French gardeners banked up in the paths against the outside of their frames for additional warmth in cold weather.

If your lot size permits it and your terrain does not necessitate arranging your growing beds along the contour for erosion control, there is an advantage in situating your beds to run on a north/ south axis. This allows the maximum amount of

**Figure 78** *Space for compost piles should be provided for easy access to the garden. Garden at the Carmel Garden Project in Virginia.*

corners left by charting your beds according to the compass. They should, however, satisfy the requirements of being easily accessible from both the path network within the garden and the vehicle access to the garden (see Figure 78). Space should also be provided for storing solar intensive and shading devices when not in use, as they often represent a considerable investment well worth taking care of.

Unfortunately, one must also plan one's garden in relation to animal pests, and a fence is an important consideration. The height and mesh of your fence will be determined by the pests in your

**Figure 79** *This whole bed is lined with chicken wire to keep out the gophers. Garden of Galen Fisher in California.*

**Figure 80** *This garden fence also serves as a tomato trellis. Garden of Kenneth and Marjorie Lauer in Pennsylvania.*

area. It is also sensible to have nets available to protect garden beds (especially berries) from birds. Fencing sometimes must be carried underground too. In one California garden, gophers were such a severe menace that the whole bed, excavated to a depth of 2 feet, is lined with 1-inch mesh chicken wire—an expensive proposition, but it works (see Figure 79). In an intensive garden one has a choice between fencing a particular bed or crop, or fencing the whole garden. Often a framework around and/or over a bed to support fencing can also support growing plants, plastic and blankets for frost protection, and a snow fence or brush for shading or wind protection (see Figures 80 and 81). A thick hedge or windbreak makes an effective fence to keep out some animals, as well as attracting to your garden predatory birds and insects that will destroy parasites harmful to your plants.

## CULTURE

Intensive gardeners are prone to making statements about how they grow two to four times as many vegetables as they used to in the same

PHOTO BY TIMOTHY FISHER.

**Figure 81** *A cucumber trellis can be used to support fall protection. Garden of Bobbie Allhouse in Vermont.*

times can help make even more effective plans for next year's garden.

Larger yields are also achieved by a much denser vegetable cover on the beds than one sees in row cultivation. In row cultivation there is one row of plants between each path, whereas in an intensive garden the equivalent of many rows of vegetables is planted between each path. The elimination of these paths allows more space in the garden for plants. Such a close and productive amount of vegetables is supported in a small area as a result of the equally intensive soil preparation.

In an intensive garden one generally prepares only the soil in the beds and walks only in the paths. In row cultivation one prepares the soil in the whole garden, then proceeds to trample a path between each row of vegetables. One gardener we spoke with calls this farming footprints. Not only is this a waste of effort, and quite possibly of fuel and fertilizer, but the soil on both sides of the row becomes compacted, which is a serious impediment to healthy root growth.

Ideally plants are spaced at such a density that the leaf tips just touch, creating a canopy through which little soil is seen between the plants. While each plant has adequate sunlight and root space, this situation creates a living mulch that shades the soil, retaining moisture and inhibiting weeds (see Figure 82). This, of course, is a difficult state to maintain, since the plants are always growing, but it is an optimal situation from which to gauge your compromises (see Figures 83 and 84).

amount of space. There are many variables in a garden situation, but, barring a raccoon invasion or similar natural calamity, you can expect to produce a lot more vegetables in an intensive garden than in a conventional garden of the same size. A well-planned scheme of successions and intercropping, calculated to make use of your entire growing season, will increase your yields. Keeping a record of planting, transplanting, and harvest

**Figure 82** *Ideally plants are spaced at a density such that they create a living mulch. Garden of Sam and Elizabeth Smith in Massachusetts.*

**Figure 83** *Dense plantings can achieve higher yields. Garden of Sam and Elizabeth Smith in Massachusetts.*

**Figure 84** *Garden of Sam and Elizabeth Smith in Massachusetts.*

PHOTO BY TIMOTY FISHER.

PHOTO BY TIMOTHY FISHER.

PHOTO BY TIMOTHY FISHER.

**Figure 85** *In this interplanting of broccoli and lettuce, the broccoli will be ready to harvest when the lettuce needs more space for continued growth. Garden at the Carmel Garden Project in Virginia.*

What must be remembered is that you are trying to maintain this optimal spacing throughout the growing season. This requires a coordinated plan. You can establish a living mulch quickly at the beginning of your growing season by using transplants and sprouted seed. This not only gives your plants a jump on the weeds, but gives you earlier harvests. When the plants in the beds begin to crowd each other, quicker maturing ones can be thinned out. A good example would be broccoli interplanted with lettuce and timed so that the lettuce would be ready to harvest just as the broccoli needed the space made available by the removal of the lettuce (see Figure 85). If, after harvesting a crop, its growing space is not needed by a neighboring plant, a succession crop should be ready to fill the space.

As you make a plan, try to visualize your garden over the whole growing season. It is under a constant plant cover, but throughout the season the specific plants are changing, growing, being harvested and replaced by new plants. The more coordinated your management of these transitions, the less abrupt they are and the more productive your garden will be.

## SPROUTING SEED

Using sprouted seed is an obvious way to extend your growing season by a few days. It also helps to assure you that you will get a plant from the seed, because you can sort out the seeds that didn't germinate before planting them. Most seeds need a fairly warm temperature to germinate, but once sprouted they will grow in less ideal circumstances. A simple sprouting technique is to lay your seeds on a moist paper towel, roll the towel up and place it in a plastic bag. Seal the bag to retain moisture and place it in a warm area. As soon as the seeds sprout, you can plant them in a flat or in the garden. It is more difficult to plant sprouted seeds than dry seed, because, being wet, they tend to clump together and you have to be careful not to break the radicals. Even if you don't go to the trouble of sprouting seeds, you can speed up the germination of most seeds simply by soaking them in water overnight before planting.

## TRANSPLANTS

Transplants are an important aspect of your intensive garden. Not only will they help you to establish a living mulch on your growing beds quickly, but they are also a way to use space efficiently (see Figure 86). For instance, you may be accustomed to planting a row of lettuce seeds, then thinning the seedlings to stand 12 inches apart. If

**Figure 86** *Transplants help to quickly establish a growing bed, using space more efficiently. In short growing seasons they are an essential step in growing long-season vegetables such as eggplants and tomatoes.*

your row is 15 feet, this will give you 15 lettuces, which occupy that space for a full six or seven weeks. If, however, you grew fifteen lettuce plants in a flat for their first four weeks, they would take up considerably less space, and in the meantime you could get a full crop of radishes from your 15-foot row.

Many people start long-season vegetables, such as tomatoes and eggplants, indoors so that their fruit will ripen before fall and cool weather comes. By starting early and transplanting some faster maturing vegetables, you can be eating them much earlier than you would otherwise. Lettuce or broccoli are good examples of this. Of course, if a seedling is not transplanted carefully, avoiding disturbance to the roots and main stem, its growth will be slowed down, eliminating any advance on the season you had been hoping to make.

The gardener with a long season and plenty of room may see little reason to spend time transplanting, yet the time spent on this may be saved on weeding and watering. The advantage in terms of weed control is that just before transplanting the soil can be turned and raked to eliminate all weeds. This gives the seedlings of your crop a good head start over the weeds, which will come later. By the time the weeds germinate (some will always still be there no matter how often you cultivate) the crop is usually well established and beginning

to form the desired living mulch to help conserve water (see Figures 87 and 88).

To grow good seedlings in flats requires a moist loose soil. A good soil for flats is made up of equal parts of compost, garden loam, and sand. A mixture of purchased potting soil and vermiculite is also very satisfactory. In order to minimize transplanting shock and encourage added growth, it is best to transplant the seedling into a richer soil than that in which it had been growing before. Plants started inside should be gradually acclimatized before transplanting outside or they will suffer shock from the temperature extremes, changes, and wind. To acclimatize or harden these plants, place them outside on warm days, but bring them in again before night. This can be done easily in a cold frame, which would be open during the day and closed at night. Gradually increase their exposure to the weather to include any day, warm nights, and eventually all the time. When they are used to the outdoor temperature, they are hardy enough to be transplanted.

## SUCCESSION

In Maine, Tony Bok maintains a weekly schedule in his commercial lettuce garden. Seeds are started in flats in a greenhouse, where they remain for two weeks, after which individual plants are

**Figure 87** *These broccoli transplants will be far ahead of any weeds that sprout now. Garden at the Carmel Garden Project in Virginia.*

**Figure 88** *Broccoli transplants and* nicotiana *at the Carmel Garden Project in Virginia.*

**Figure 89**  *Succession lettuce plantings in the garden of Sam and Elizabeth Smith in Maine.*

PHOTO BY TIMOTHY FISHER.

transplanted into larger flats with more space. When the plants are four weeks old, they are pricked out into the garden beds, spaced one foot apart. Once a week Tony fertilizes all the lettuces with diluted cow urine from his small dairy. Each week he begins this process again, and so has a constant supply of young lettuce plants to take the place of those harvested from the garden. Though dealing with only one crop, this example illustrates how succession planting can help you to utilize your entire growing area to the maximum. The growing season is stretched to include four weeks' growth inside the greenhouse before it is warm enough for outdoor planting, and could be extended at the other end of the season with the use of solar intensive devices.

Succession planting means that when one crop is harvested, there will be a succeeding crop planted to take its place. The purpose of this is to keep the garden in continual production, thus giving the greatest yields per area. Whether planting seeds or seedlings, a productive intensive schedule will include succession planting. Since different vegetables and varieties of vegetables are suited to different seasons and conditions, succession planting can take advantage of this by starting cool weather crops in the spring, followed by warm crops midsummer and cool crops again for the fall (see Figure 90). With quick-maturing vegetables you may fit several successions into a single season. Even when growing long-season vegetables that require the full season to mature, it is a good practice to succeed them with a winter cover crop such as winter rye (see Figure 91). The cover crop will

PHOTO BY TIMOTHY FISHER.

**Figure 90**  *Carrots and broccoli thrive in the autumn garden of Timothy and Kathleen Fisher in Vermont.*

**Figure 91**  *A cover crop of winter rye.*

PHOTO BY PAUL DOSCHER.

hold the soil, preventing erosion during the winter, and can be tilled in as green manure in the spring.

Succession planting is often combined with intercropping (growing two or more crops together). If possible, you should include crop rotation principles in your succession planting.

## CROP ROTATIONS

Different vegetables take different nutrients in varying amounts from the soil. Some plants also enrich the soil's store of nutrients. In order to maintain a balance in the soil it is necessary to grow different plants from year to year in each of your garden beds.

There are some deep-rooted plants capable of loosening the soil, some bringing mineral nutrients up from the subsoil. Alfalfa and buckwheat are often noted for their ability to do this. It is not clear whether they allow those nutrients to be used by other plants immediately, but as the roots decompose, and if these plants are green manured or composted, the nutrients will later become available.

In planning rotations vegetables are usually divided into groups, according to how much they take from the soil. The group called heavy feeders draw larger quantities of macronutrients (particularly nitrogen) from the soil to grow large quantities of foliage or large fruits. Light feeders, generally legumes or root crops, withdraw fewer nutrients and are usually plants of less physical mass.

Legumes are classed as light feeders because their presence can increase the soil's supply of nitrogen. This is due to the ability of bacterial nodules that live on the roots of leguminous plants to convert nitrogen in the air into a form usable by plants in the soil. The roots of the legumes then absorb this nitrogen from the bacteria. Frequently, however, vegetable legumes like peas or green beans are not carried through a long enough life cycle in the garden to contribute a significant amount of nitrogen. In addition to their ability to fix nitrogen, deep-rooted legumes such as clover and alfalfa are able to bring calcium and phosphorus up from deeper levels in the soil.

Nonleguminous light feeders are mostly bulb or root crops, including turnips, parsnips, carrots, radishes, and beets. Heavy feeders include corn, potatoes, eggplants, peppers, squash, melons, the cabbage family (especially cauliflower), lettuce, spinach, chard, and celery. A useful rotation possible in an intensive garden would be a heavy feeder such as corn, followed by legumes such as soybeans, followed by a light feeder such as carrots.

Your rotation should make certain that a bed planted in heavy feeders will be followed in succession by light feeders. This succession can occur in one growing season, or from one year to the next. If you grow grains, they should be incorporated into the rotation too, as well as cover and green manure crops. If you have a limited supply of organic fertilizer, such as manure, then including a leguminous cover crop (clover, alfalfa, vetch, etc.) in your rotation will be very important.

Crop rotation is a big aid in maintaining a healthy soil balance, but it won't satisfy all your soil needs. You will need to continue your other soil maintenance practices too.

Diseases and insects that cause crop damage are usually partial to a specific genus or species and can often remain over winter in the soil. Used as a sanitary measure, crop rotation can minimize the damage they do. If the same crop or crop family (for example, any of the many members of the cabbage tribe) is planted in the same soil two or more years in a row, then your pest population will increase, and your problems are likely to get worse each year. The idea is to starve out diseases and harmful insects by depriving them of their chosen host plants. The severity of this problem will vary with your local situation, but if you play it safe by rotating your crops, you can expect healthier plants and soil.

## INTERCROPPING

The importance of intercropping, or the practice of growing two or more crops together, in the intensive garden is to obtain the maximum number of individual plants within each bed while avoid-

**Figure 92** *Interplanting can be easily handled by planting rows within garden beds. Garden of Timothy and Kathleen Fisher in Vermont.*

ing the ill effects of overcrowding (see Figures 92 and 93). The best vegetables to interplant are those that make opposite or complementary demands upon the soil, water supply, and available sunlight, or that supply each other with particular advantages such as support or shade.

A heavy feeding vegetable and a light feeding one, planted next to each other, can offer the soil-balancing effects of crop rotation at once rather than over a period of time. Of course, sequential

**Figure 93** *Intercropping of celery, lettuce, and beets in the garden of Drew and Louise Langsner in North Carolina.*

crop rotation will still be important in the intercropped garden to combat disease and pest problems.

Theoretically, the optimum planting scheme for interplanting is a grid on which every other plant is a heavy or light feeder. This works very well when the sizes of plants grown together are relatively close, such as lettuce and carrots. John Jeavons, writing about his California gardening experience, has evidently had good results using such a grid plan based on hexagons. But one has to be pragmatic. In New England, where we try to grow the majority of our year's vegetables in the few summer months (the same months during which most other outdoor endeavors must be accomplished), we tend to choose a simpler system. Alternating rows, bands, or blocks of heavy and light feeding vegetables make a very satisfactory intercropping layout.

Though the principle of intercropping heavy and light feeders is sound, it has to be accompanied by knowledge of the individual vegetables involved. For instance, it sounds great to grow squash and perhaps beets together, but squash has a tendency to take over everything in sight, covering paths and shading all competition; what began as an intercrop ends as a squash patch with a few shaded, stunted beets. The moral of this is to give squash plenty of room or its plant neighbors will soon discover what unfair competition is all about. We usually plant squash in beds at the edge of the garden and encourage them to spread away from the rest of the garden. One way to deal with unruly squash is to buy seed for the bush-type varieties. We have found them to be productive and much tamer. There are things that can be interplanted with squash, of course, and pole beans seem fairly obvious, so long as the beans have started up their poles before the squash starts covering the countryside.

It is well known that the American Indians grew corn, squash, and beans together. This is an obvious combination, in which the beans can help to supply the nitrogen the squash and corn so voraciously consume. The beans and squash grow in the space between the corn, which would otherwise be uncovered soil and subject to erosion. Their leaves shade the soil, lessening water evaporation, and the beans' taproots use nutrients and water that the corn and squash cannot reach. The beans should get plenty of sunlight while the corn is still relatively small, though they may be shaded somewhat by the time the corn grows fairly large. Ideally, the beans would be harvested before the corn, and this shading would not be a problem.

This method sounds great and in many cases is, particularly with a bush-type bean. However, we have also seen garden disasters planted with all the right intentions. Cases in which the corn growth outpaced the beans altogether resulted in zero beans. The problems can be worked out with practice, observing and adjusting planting times in relation to one another.

In some situations sturdy, tall plants are planted with climbing plants to serve as a living trellis for the climbers. Corn and sunflowers are often planted to support pole beans or cucumbers. Some gardeners are great proponents of this idea, but it takes careful timing, spacing, and planting. Take the same corn and beans interplanting example again, only using pole beans instead of bush beans. It works very well for some gardeners, but we have also seen the pole beans get ahead of the corn, which continued to grow, but was so strangled and shaded that it produced few good corncobs. By the time the beans were ready to pick they had grown into such a corn-intertwined jungle that many of them could not be reached at all. As you see, one has to think through an interplanting to its possible conclusions. For some crops it may be more practical to follow a more traditional crop rotation.

Shading can work both for you or against you, too, when you're interplanting. Shade-tolerant (or cool weather crops in midsummer) plants will thrive in the shade of a taller plant, whereas in another situation the shade of a tall plant will be very detrimental to the shorter plant. In general, if an undercrop is being forced to grow abnormally tall and spindly, or fails to develop its normal green coloring, you have left the shading crop in the garden too long or planted it too densely. Cucumbers are often suggested as a good midsummer understory crop, since they like both heat and some shade. But heat is relative; in northeastern Vermont our summer is cool enough that we find cucumbers need the full sunlight to prosper.

A limited water supply may be another reason for intercropping. An assortment of vegetables at different stages of maturity will not all require their peak amounts of water at the same time, so water needs per bed will be more balanced.

Intercropping is probably the most useful to the intensive gardener when coordinated with succession planting. In this situation the intercropped vegetables are timed to be at different stages of development because they were either planted or transplanted at different times. For example, one might plant lettuce in the spring with radishes. When the radishes are pulled, tall peas could be planted in their stead. By the time the peas reach an appreciable height the season will have warmed enough that their shade can benefit the nearly mature lettuces. In many ways an overlapping succession like this is the easiest way to manage intercropping. Because the peak growth of the plants growing together does not coincide, direct competition can usually be avoided. Seed packets give information about the number of days to maturity of the given vegetable. Use this information to schedule successions.

Difficulties with succession intercropping come when the timing is not coordinated. If two intercrops are coming to maturity at the same time, both may need more space, though neither is ready to harvest. All you can do is let them be crowded and get inferior produce, or thin them out and get less food than you anticipated. You will know next time to schedule the planting times of the two plants farther apart or to allow more space between plants.

Besides all of these other possible benefits, interplanting can mean a wider variety of plant growth and habitat for spiders and insect predators, which can be a valuable control of destructive insect populations in your garden. Nature creates complex interrelationships between living organisms of great diversity. This diversity gives natural systems a flexibility that enables them to recover amazingly from natural disasters and the insults of humanity. Imitating this diversity and complexity in your garden is certainly an important step toward growing food in a way that complements and respects the processes of nature.

## COMPANION PLANTING

Companion planting, like intercropping, is based upon the natural interactions of plants used for the benefit of the gardener. Companion planting includes intercropping, but carries these principles further, dealing with plant interactions that are much subtler, more variable, and more experimental. Most of the research into companion planting has been done by biodynamic gardeners and farmers; hence, most of what we know about the subject comes from them. "The Bio-dynamic Method of farming is based on the study of (and a steadily expanding knowledge about) the mutual influences of living organisms."[1]

These mutual influences are the basis of companion planting. Plants have been found to like, dislike, or respond indifferently toward neighboring plants (see Figure 94). These relationships should have a direct bearing upon how well various plants will grow. For example, leeks and celery are both supposed to benefit from being close to each other, whereas beans and onions are supposed to suffer ill effects from being planted together. In other relationships one species may benefit or suffer, while its companion appears unaffected.

Companion planting is also used to attract or discourage insects. Nature has endowed many plants with mechanisms designed to insure survival, and pest attacks are an important threat to a species' ability to survive. Using plants that have developed an ability to repel certain insects is a logical way to promote a healthy garden environment. However, it is important to remember that many of nature's mechanisms are very subtle, and what works in one situation may not in another. Variances in soil, climate, nutrients, plant varieties, and different periods of their life cycle, all affect the ability of plants to repel pests.

Few gardeners have consistent experiences with companion planting as a pest deterrent. The most commonly used plants for this purpose seem to be

[1] Helen Philbrick and Richard B. Gregg. *Companion Plants & How to Use Them* (Old Greenwich, Conn.: The Devin–Adair Company, 1966), p. xi.

*How to Use the Chart*

This chart is designed to be a handy reference for garden planning. As you are preparing to lay out your intensive garden, some quick glances at the chart can indicate which plants may work well as companions and which may not.

Use it like the mileage chart on a road map. Simply find the name of the plant you are concerned with, and look across its row and down its column to identify its possible relationship to the other plants on the chart.

*The Symbols*

● Indicates that two plants are mutual companions. It is possible that they will both benefit from being planted next to each other.

→ Indicates that one plant likes the other, but only one of the two may clearly benefit from the relationship. i.e. beans are reported to benefit from being planted near carrots so the arrow points toward carrots.

🐛 Indicates one of the two plants may deter or repel a particular insect pest. In most cases this symbol is associated with a plant which repels a pest from another crop.

✗ Indicates these plants are antagonists. Placing these plants together may be detrimental to either or both of them. In general antagonists should not follow each other in succession planting either.

The blank spaces on the chart indicate that either no companion/antagonist relationship has been identified between the two plants involved or that no one has yet studied the relationship. If you have experience with pairs which are not shown on the chart, you can add your information in the blank spaces.

For more detailed information on companion planting relationships consult one of the following books:

*Companion Plants and How to Use Them* by Helen Philbrick and Richard Gregg (Greenwich, Ct.: Devon–Adair Company, 1966).
*Secrets of Companion Planting for Successful Gardening* by Louise Riotte (Charlotte, Vt.: Garden Way, 1975).
*How to Grow More Vegetables* by John Jeavons (Berkeley, Calif.: Ten Speed Press, 1979).
*Getting the Most from Your Garden* by the Editors of *Organic Gardening* magazine (Emmaus, Pa.: Rodale Press, 1980).

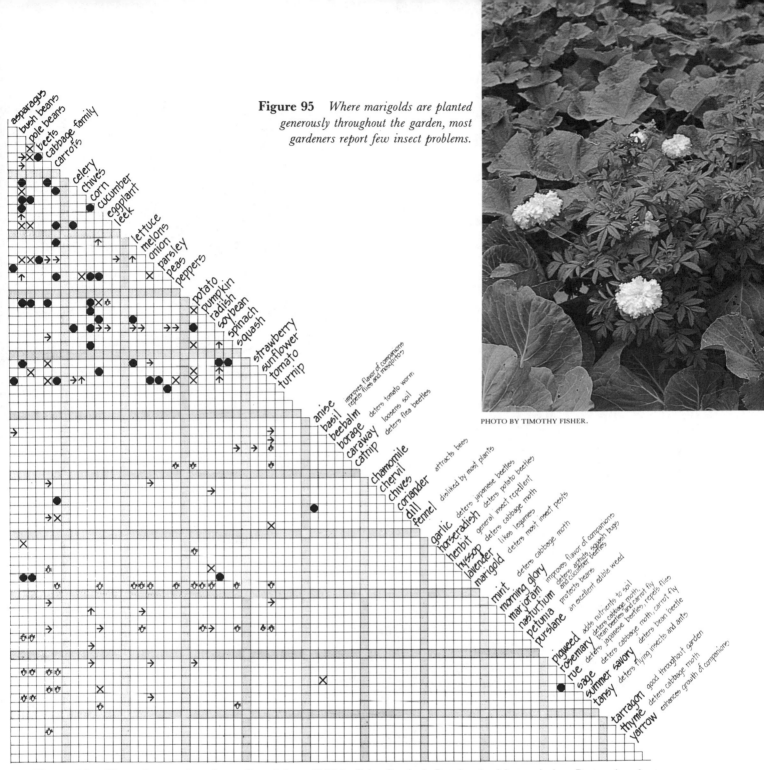

**Figure 95** *Where marigolds are planted generously throughout the garden, most gardeners report few insect problems.*

PHOTO BY TIMOTHY FISHER.

**Figure 94** *Chart of companion plants. Copyright © 1978 by Solar Survival. Reprinted with permission. Poster size charts are available from Solar Survival, Box 275, Harrisville, New Hampshire 03450.*

marigolds, nasturtiums, and members of the onion family.

A root excretion produced by both French and African marigolds has been proven to be toxic to soil nematodes. Apparently it is most effective when the plants are green manured, but it also works while the plants are growing. Many gardeners grow marigolds because they believe that the odor is an effective repellent for bean beetles, whiteflies, and aphids. Where marigolds are planted generously throughout the garden most gardeners report few insect problems (see Figure

95). Additional scientific research shows that marigolds may also be useful in controlling fusarium and verticillium bacteria in the soil.

Nasturtiums are supposed to deter whiteflies, aphids, and squash bugs. Some people report that this is true, while others have watched their squash plants wither into skeletons surrounded by mounds of luxuriant nasturtiums. Alas, that is the state of companion planting at this point in time. We know far too little to practice it effectively on a consistent basis.

Garlic and onions are renowned for discouraging garden pests and are interplanted with members of the cabbage family in the hope that they will repel cabbage worms (the larvae of a small white butterfly). Some experts speculate that this is only an effective measure when the larvae stage coincides with the time of the onions' flowering.

**Figure 96** *Flowers like borage attract bees and help to insure pollination of fruiting vegetables such as squashes, cucumbers, and peppers. Garden of Bobbie Allhouse in Vermont.*

PHOTO BY TIMOTHY FISHER.

PHOTO BY TIMOTHY FISHER.

**Figure 97** *When a vegetable plant dies in his Maine garden, Tony Bok replaces it with a flower.*

There is, however, also evidence that certain substances in onion skins have a suppressive effect on some soil-borne parasites and diseases.

Many plants require insect pollination for fruit development. Honey bees are generally credited with performing much of the pollination of garden crops, but many other insects do this also. Certainly any flower that serves to attract large numbers of bees will be a benefit to insect-pollinated, fruiting garden plants such as melon, squashes, cucumbers, tomatoes, peppers, etc. Many flowering herbs are seen in gardens for this purpose, including borage, coriander, and catnip (see Figures 96 and 97).

Companion planting, it is claimed, can also enhance the flavor of vegetables. This is hard to substantiate, for taste is a difficult thing to evaluate objectively. In general, the advice for this kind of companion planting seems to follow a scheme of planting together what you like to eat and cook together.

In spite of all the "ifs" involved in this account of companion planting for pest control and flavor improvement, we have confidence in the principles of the idea. Still, it is hardly a complete area of study, and there is not enough knowledge to insure success. Just as in any planting scheme you use, keeping a record of what you grow where, when, and with what other plants will turn out to be your most valuable garden planning resource.

## SPACING

Spacing between plants is one of the most important aspects in which intensive culture differs from row or field culture. Spacing will vary according to your climate and the sizes plants attain in that climate. Obviously this will take experience and time to know. You will probably adjust the spacings recommended here by your experience. For instance, you may plant eggplants 18 inches apart and find that in your situation they don't fill the full 18 inches. In the Northeast, where the weather is often moist, close planting can cause rot at ground level in lettuce, for example. If you have a damp or cool garden, this is something to be aware of.

The general goal in spacing is that the leaf tips of neighboring plants, when mature, will just touch. Spacing tables given here will approximate the space needed by one mature plant. These are only guidelines, as spacing will vary considerably with soil, climate, and vegetables.

If you are growing two intercrops that will be maturing at the same time, you can determine their spacing by adding the individual spacings together and dividing by two. Things can be spaced closer if you plan to use interplanted, overlapping successions. This is because the intercropped vegetables in a bed, say, of lettuce and cauliflower will be planned not to reach maturity at the same time. Thus, while full spaces must be left for one of the plants, the other will be less than full size, so less space need be allowed. The larger plant will, as has been discussed before, be harvested, allowing space for the younger plants to grow to maturity (see Figure 98). This cycle can be continued by transplanting small seedlings into the spaces where the first maturing plants were harvested; these will grow, and when the second crop is taken off the bed, the third one will fill in again. It goes without saying that this sort of coordination takes careful planning to succeed and that factors of weather could change the most well-laid plans. Only experience will be able to tell you how best this may be done in your situation.

Your spacing may also vary depending upon

**Figure 98**  *This mature cabbage should be harvested to give the growing lettuce more room. Garden at the New Alchemy Institute in Massachusetts.*

how you will use or harvest your crop. For example, we generally broadcast lettuce in a bed and tear off handfuls of leaves when we need them for a salad. If we were marketing lettuce, we would probably choose to use the same 10- to 12-inch spacing popular with the commercial growers we visited, since the wide spacing produces shapely plants that can be uprooted and sold as heads.

To determine spacing for vegetables not included in this chart a general spacing guide is to use the recommended distance between plants in the row printed on the seed packet. Space plants that distance apart in every direction, ignoring the recommended distances between rows.

## SUGGESTED SPACING BETWEEN THE CENTERS OF MATURE PLANTS

(given in inches)

| | |
|---|---|
| Asparagus | 12 |
| Beans, bush | 6–8 |
| Beans, pole | 4–6 plants per pole, 18 inches apart |
| Beets | 3–6 |
| Broccoli | 12–18 |
| Brussels sprouts | 14–16 |
| Cabbage, Chinese | 10–12 |
| Cabbage, regular | 15–18 |

SUGGESTED SPACING (*Cont.*)

| | |
|---|---|
| Carrots | 2–3 |
| Cauliflower | 12–15 |
| Celery | 6 |
| Chard | 6–8 |
| Corn | 12–18 |
| Cucumbers | 8–12 |
| Eggplant | 14–18 |
| Garlic | 3–4 |
| Kale | 12 |
| Kohlrabi | 4–8 |
| Leeks | 3–5 |
| Lettuce, head | 12 |
| Lettuce, leaf | 6–12 |
| Melons | 12–14 |
| Mustard greens | 6 |
| Onions | 3–6 |
| Parsley | 4–5 |
| Parsnips | 3–4 |
| Peas, bush | 3–4 |
| Peas, climbing | 3–4 |
| Peppers | 10–16 |
| Potatoes | 10–14 |
| Pumpkin | 24–30 |
| Radishes | 1–2 |
| Rhubarb | 6–8 |
| Rutabagas | 6 |
| Salsify | 2–4 |
| Scallions | 1 |
| Spinach, New Zealand | 10–12 |
| Spinach, regular | 4–6 |
| Squash, summer and zucchini | 20–36 |
| Squash, winter | 26–30 |
| Sunflowers | 12–24 |
| Tomatoes | 18–24 |
| Turnips | 2–4 |
| Watermelons | 20–24 |

## SEED SELECTION

Choosing seed suited to the climate and season you will be gardening in can make a big difference and help you to utilize fringe ends of the season. The ideal, of course, is to get varieties of vegetables that will mature from seed within the length of your growing season. This is impossible with some vegetables in many places (such as tomatoes, peppers, and eggplant in New England). This will make it necessary for you to start plants indoors or in solar intensive devices before your growing season has actually begun. Of course it is easy to get seedlings from a nursery if you find raising them yourself difficult or unnecessary. The advantage of starting your own is that you have a much wider choice among varieties in buying seeds than in buying plants.

On the other end of things you can expect to get more than one crop of quick-growing vegetables like spinach, peas, and lettuce. Some varieties of these grow best in the cool of spring and fall, but dislike the heat or dryness of summer, while other varieties may be much more tolerant of summer weather. Selecting which variety to plant during different stages of the growing season can go a long way toward giving you a continuous supply of these fresh vegetables.

You can economize on space in your garden by choosing seed for compact varieties, when available, of the vegetables you plan to grow. Some compact types are probably developed more as novelties than for food production, so read the catalog or seed packet carefully.

If you have never grown vegetables in your area before, it would be helpful to ask neighboring gardeners what varieties they have had success with. It may also be to your advantage to purchase your seed from seed companies located in a similar climate to yours. A seed that grows to maturity in fifty days in one climate may grow more quickly or slowly in your location.

A last consideration is whether you hope to save your own seed. If this is so, the seed you select initially will have to be open-pollinated rather than hybrid. Hybrid seed does not always produce a plant true to its parent.

# INTENSIVE GARDENING METHODS

Timothy Fisher and Kathleen Kolb

WHILE VISITING intensive gardens in the eastern United States we were impressed with the diversity of methods successfully employed in preparing garden beds. The gardeners we met had adapted intensive techniques creatively to many individual locations and needs. In recognition of this diversity we will describe a variety of these gardens, with the hope that you can gain from them as you evolve a method best suited to your situation and personality.

The growing beds in most intensive gardens are permanent, meaning they are in the same place every year. The obvious advantages to this are that the majority of the work in establishing a garden is done the first year. Thereafter, preparing the bed is a much smaller chore. The gardener adds his compost, etc., to the same bed areas each year rather than broadcasting it across an entire garden, including areas to be used for paths. Thus he takes advantage of all the work and organic matter put into the bed the previous season.

Our garden in northern Vermont is comprised of permanent beds. We use beds boxed with boards to provide maximum use of the deep-dug area, to eliminate erosion, and because they look tidy. The boards also provide a barrier to weeds encroaching from the paths. This is most effective if the boards extend a few inches below the level of the paths. A mixture of grass and clover is grown in the paths, which are mown as part of the surrounding lawn. In addition to being attractive, the grass paths prevent erosion and create a soft ground cover between the beds that is neither muddy nor dried out (see Figure 99).

The beds themselves are dug by hand (see Figure 100). Sod, weeds (and pernicious weed rhizomes), and many rocks are removed from the soil in excavating the bed area to a two-foot depth. Then wood ashes, compost, manure, and rock phosphate are mixed with the loosened soil. Though this is done fairly casually, the average addition is a wheelbarrow load of manure and one of compost per 25 square feet, and a few shovelsful of ashes and rock phosphate. For certain crops not nearly so much is added, while others get a higher share (see Chapter 2 for more detailed fertilizer information). The bed area is boxed with 10-inch-high boards and filled with this fortified soil to create small, level plateaus of rich, aerated earth. Though it initially requires a lot of work to establish these beds, they need little maintenance during the growing season and are given only a cur-

**Figure 99**   *The Allhouse's garden in northeastern Vermont has permanent grass paths between the garden beds.*

**Figure 100**   *Our beds are excavated to a depth of two feet; sod, weeds, and rocks are removed; the loosened soil is returned to the beds with the addition of wood ashes, compost, manure, and rock phosphate.*

sory turning, with the addition of organic matter and necessary fertilizer, each subsequent spring. Some people will find such deep soil preparation unnecessary, but in our situation it is worthwhile, if only because some of the rocks we have removed take up nearly half the area of our smaller beds (3½ feet by 7 feet).

The biggest work-saver for us in establishing a new bed is to lay salvaged sheets of corrugated metal roofing over the area where the bed will be. This is done a full year before digging the bed. The next spring the soil under the roofing is free of weeds and sod, and allows very easy digging. Because we have them available, we use scrap hardwood boards to box in our beds. Though these have lasted well for five years, they are beginning to show signs of age. Concrete blocks or cast slabs offer greater permanence. We also hope to make bed sides out of styrofoam insulation covered with ferrocement. These should provide the insulation needed for solar intensive devices plus the permanence of concrete. Some people have expressed a concern that wood sides on beds harbor slugs. Though none of the gardeners with boxed beds whom we visited have had problems with this, it is definitely a possibility.

Intensive beds do not need to be permanent to be successful. Betsy Hibbard in Pennsylvania alternates her beds and paths each year. She uses a garden fork to form six parallel beds. Throughout the season the paths between beds are sheet-composted with leaves, grass clippings, or similar coverings. The following spring soil from the beds is forked on top of the composted paths to form new beds, and paths remain where the previous year's beds were. The new paths are sheet-composted to become beds the following year.

At the New Alchemy Institute on Cape Cod they practice a similar method on a much larger scale. Four-foot-wide beds are laid out with one-foot-wide paths between them. The paths are dug out to a depth of 6 to 12 inches, and this soil is spread on the beds. The New Alchemists then sheet-compost, gradually filling the paths through the season with any available organic matter. Gardener Hilde Maingay points out that this method is more efficient, since compost materials are moved only once, and garden weeds and wastes can simply be thrown into the paths as one weeds or harvests. Also, their garden is designed as a prototype for a suburban situation, where there are seldom enough materials at one time to make a

68

full compost pile, and where neighbors may complain that a compost pile is ugly. Other advantages are that nutrient leaching occurs where you want it to occur in the garden; the water-holding capacity of the soil in the beds is noticeably improved; the sheet composting replaces the need to mulch the paths and sides of beds; and the beds remain moister than with mulch. In this system the paths could be flooded for irrigation, in which case the water would be enriched with nutrients from the paths (see Figure 101).

Hilde mentions that it requires careful maneuvering to deliver and distribute this organic matter to the narrow paths. She writes:

> Sheet composting still does not completely replace the regular compost pile. In a well-built, balanced pile the heat created during the first decomposition process can kill grubs, eggs, and some pathogenic organisms. In the next steps of the breakdown process, the action of fungi produces antibiotics and growth hormones in higher concentration than possible in

**Figure 101** *Hilde Maingay sheet composts the paths in the garden at the New Alchemy Institute in Massachusetts. The beds are moved one-third of their width each year, so the sheet composted material becomes part of the garden bed.*

PHOTO BY TIMOTHY FISHER.

regular soil. . . . At the end of the growing season all the beds were moved a third of their width by digging up part of the beds and putting dirt on top of the sheet compost filled pathways. At the same time new pathways were created.[1]

After four years the beds will have shifted to their original locations (see Figure 102). With the great quantity of organic matter composting in the paths, Hilde says, they have no worries about compacting paths that will next year be part of the beds. The vitality we saw in the garden certainly suggests no such problems.

[1] Hilde Maingay. "Intensive Vegetable Production," *Journal of the New Alchemists,* No. 4 (Woods Hole, Massachusetts: 1977), p. 48.

first year

**Figure 102** *The New Alchemy Institute's system for sheet composting in the paths between garden beds means that the beds move one-third of their width every year.*

second year

third year

fourth year

**Figure 103**  *The late Alan Chadwick's gardens in Virginia (Carmel in the Valley) use double-digging to form their beds.*

**Figure 104**  *Garden of the late Alan Chadwick in Virginia (Carmel in the Valley).*

## TILTH AND CULTIVATION METHODS

There is debate among intensive gardeners whether it is best to dig beds by hand, use a roto-tiller, or do no tilling at all. We have seen good gardens in which all three methods have been used.

The gardening techniques used by the late Alan Chadwick have been popularized in America by John Jeavons in his book *How to Grow More Vegetables*.[2] The method goes by the name of biodynamic/French intensive gardening,[3] and relies on hand digging to supply tilth. The garden beds are cultivated by double-digging, which is an old technique for preparing garden soil and is still common in ornamental horticulture (see Figures 103–105). Chadwick's method generally is first to skim vegetation off the growing bed with a sharp spade and set it aside. A trench is dug across the bed one "spit" (the height of a spade's blade) deep and the soil removed. Next, a spading fork is pushed into the soil at the bottom of the trench and worked and twisted around so that the soil is thoroughly loosened without being removed.

---

[2] John Jeavons. *How to Grow More Vegetables* (Berkeley, California: Ten Speed Press, 1979).

[3] Although this method is called biodynamic/French intensive gardening, it derives only selected aspects from both systems.

**Figure 105**  *Double digging.*

1. *Skim vegetation from the bed surface and open a trench as deep as your shovel.*

2. *Loosen the subsoil in the trench.*

3. *Put the skimmed vegetation in the trench.*

4. *Fill the first trench as you open the next one, continuing in the same manner.*

70

Then the weeds or plant residues that had been skimmed off are put into the trench. They are covered with soil removed in the process of opening the adjacent trench. In opening the second trench, the digging becomes "double slide digging," for the soil is cut in chunks and tossed (or "slid") onto the layer of vegetation in such a way that the soil retains its natural stratification, top on top and bottom on bottom. Though loosened, the soil basically holds together without crumbling. After this basic preparation compost and manure are added in a separate process, being turned into the top inches of the bed.

There are circumstances in which you might accomplish this digging differently, by what Chadwick terms "double turn digging." By this method vegetation is not skimmed from the soil. Rather than carefully maintaining the topsoil strata in their original relation, as in double slide digging, the top spit of soil, including vegetation, is inverted. This may be useful in several situations, as when you have a problem with surface-breeding insects damaging your plants. If, in an older bed, you wanted to deliver the organic matter that has accumulated near the soil surface to a lower level for root crops, etc., you could use double turn digging. In general, though, this is not recommended ". . . because it destroys the health of the surface soil."[4] To save time in digging large areas, these may be single dug, without fork-loosening the subsoil. If you have such a heavy subsoil that it defies forking, you may also single dig. There are other circumstances that might cause you to alter the manner in which you cultivate your beds. A few of them are described in Tom Cuthbertson's book, *Alan Chadwick's Enchanted Garden.*

In *How to Grow More Vegetables* John Jeavons mentions that the digging process is best when the soil is moist—neither wet, in which case it would compact, nor dry, which might turn it to a fine dust. Rather than adding soil amendments in a separate operation, Jeavons describes applying them to the surface before the actual digging commences; they will probably mix with the surface soil as it is loosened.

[4] Tom Cuthbertson, *Alan Chadwick's Enchanted Garden* (New York: E.P. Dutton, 1978), p. 168.

Chadwick's methods (as described by John Jeavons) were followed successfully by many of the gardeners we visited, and the gardens founded by Alan Chadwick at Carmel in the Valley in Virginia are an inspiration to any gardener. However, many of the people we visited in New England found the work involved in double-digging the beds unnecessary.

Dr. Frank Eggert of the University of Maine at Orono is in the fourth year of a five-year comparison study of five different soil treatments.[5] All the organic plots (chemically fertilized plots were also studied) were given the same quantities of fertilizer. There was no significant, consistent difference in yields of marketable produce between plots that were double-dug according to Jeavons's specifications and those given only a surface tilling with a rototiller. The labor difference, however, was significant. It took three to four hours to double-dig each 100-square-foot plot in preparation for seeding the Jeavons-type bed, whereas it took two to four minutes to rototill each other plot of 100 square feet. Dr. Eggert points out that there is a notable difference in climate between the area of California where Jeavons's research has been done and New England. In the California area the ground never freezes, the soil is disturbed only by man, and there is low rainfall. "This technique may be valid in California, but here the soil is frozen in the winter to four feet, it heaves and settles a lot." He feels the frost action loosens the subsoil adequately to eliminate the need for deep- or double-digging garden beds in his northern climate.

## MACHINE TILLING

Many intensive gardeners find a rototiller an invaluable tool. Many other gardeners who now use hand tilling or no tilling found a rototiller an aid when originally establishing their beds. All the

[5] Five different soil treatments are being tested in this study at the University of Maine. There are three test sites, each of which is divided into twenty-five plots. Five plots of each soil treatment are distributed throughout each test site. The treatments are: (a) biodynamic/French intensive (as described by John Jeavons); (b) commercial fertilizer; (c) commercial fertilizer plus seaweed extract spray; (d) organic and (e) organic plus mulch.

**Figure 106** *Paul and Debbie Doscher use a rear-tined tiller and furrowing tool to build their beds.*

commercial intensive gardeners we visited relied upon some rototilling or the use of larger machinery, finding hand tilling too time-consuming to be profitable. They relied upon green manure crops as part of their fertility program, and found a rototiller indispensable for tilling these crops into the soil.

In author Doscher's southern New Hampshire garden a rototiller is used both to form and cultivate beds. One method of forming beds when no subsoil loosening is desired makes use of a rear-tined tiller and furrowing tool (see Figures 106–107). First, the entire garden area is tilled to as deep a level as possible (usually 6 to 8 inches).

Then the furrower is attached to the tiller and run across the area wherever paths will be located. The furrower pushes the soil up onto surrounding areas, forming instant beds after only one or two passes. The beds are then leveled with a rake.

The Doschers have also used the tiller in subsoiling. First, with a cultivating fork and shovel they pull aside the topsoil from a bed already built or a new bed area. The soil is raked into long mounds on either side of the bed, revealing the subsoil. They then run the tiller down into the subsoil, loosening and turning it to a depth of 8 to 10 inches. Next, the topsoil is pushed back over the subsoil, with care not to mix the two layers. The bed is finally re-formed and allowed to settle for a few days before planting.

Adam Tomash in Maine uses a walking tractor with furrower attachment to deep-dig his market garden in preparation for carrots. He makes a preliminary pass with the furrower where the wide-row carrot plantings will be, leaving approximately 6-inch-deep trenches in the wake of the furrower and ridges of earth between the trenches. Adam often adds compost to these trenches. He next offsets the position of his furrower on the walking tractor by half the track width of the tractor. With the furrower offset he digs new trenches where the ridges of earth were, pushing both the ridges and the soil from the new trenches on top of the original trench. By this method Adam builds narrow raised beds, which are loosened and enriched to a depth of approximately 12 inches. As determined by the 24-inch width of his walking tractor the raised beds are about 12 inches wide.

George Crane, a commercial vegetable grower in Vermont, had a bed-forming attachment built to his specifications and mounts it on the 3-point

**Figure 107** *A rear-tine rototiller with a furrowing attachment can be used to form beds in new gardens. First the area is cultivated to the full depth (usually about 8″) and then the tiller with furrower is used to push soil up from the path areas on to the beds. A rake is used to finish the beds.* Photo courtesy of Garden Way, maker of *Troy-Bilt*® Tillers, Troy, New York 12180.

hitch behind his tractor. The tractor straddles one four-foot-wide bed with its wheels, forming the paths between beds. George's bed-forming system is coordinated with the machinery he uses for planting, surface cultivating, spraying, and harvesting.

Before making the beds, the soil is cultivated. The final cultivation involves rotovating the full area with a 36-tine, 60-inch-wide (the same width as the tractor) rotovator to the depth of 12 inches.[6] To permit rotovating to this depth, the field must be free of rocks. To minimize soil compaction George uses a lightweight tractor for rotovating and bed forming.

The bed-forming frame works as follows (see Figure 108). A disk is mounted behind and just inside of each rear tractor tire. Each disk (from a heavy-duty disk harrow) is adjustable in angle and depth, but usually is mounted at an angle of about 45 degrees to the direction the tractor is moving in. The disks scoop into the loose soil, forming the sides of the bed and pushing the soil toward hardwood forming boards (also adjusted at about 45

[6] A rotovator is a wide rototiller that attaches to the rear of a tractor, running off the tractor's power take-off.

degrees) which spread the soil across the bed. Behind the forming boards a hardwood flattening board stretches the width of the frame to smooth the bed surface. At the back of the frame 40 small disks give the soil a final pulverization to break up any small clumps and leave a fine seedbed.

The height of the beds is adjustable by means both of the three-point hitch and the individual parts. George normally makes the surface of his beds about 8 inches above the tractor wheel path. The soil in the beds is loose to a depth that usually enables him to push his arm into the soil up to his elbow.

## MINIMAL TILLING

Frank Eggert, who finds a rototiller valuable for seedbed preparation and controlling early weeds, cautions that soil should not be tilled any more than is necessary. Tilling destroys the soil's structure, and a gardener should be trying to improve this structure.

A loose rich soil can be built and maintained with no tilling by either hand or machine. We vis-

**Figure 108** *A tractor-drawn bed-former.*

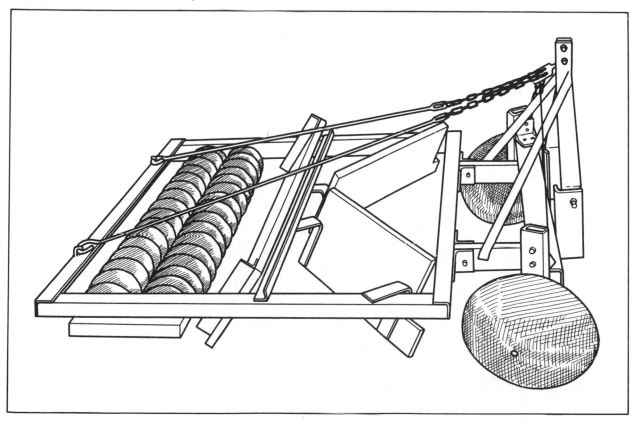

**Figure 109** *David Emery's no-till garden in Maine.*

ited the very productive garden of David Emery in Maine, which has been managed organically for twenty-five years. He adds up to a foot of mulch to the garden each year, but never tills (see Figure 109). When he wants to plant, he simply pulls apart enough mulch to allow him to scratch the soil with his finger and drop in the seed.

To establish raised beds, Janney Munsell, also of Maine, used a rototiller on her garden area (see Figure 110). Then, on the loose soil she laid out bottomless boxes to contain her raised beds and shoveled the loose topsoil from the paths into the beds, filling the boxes to the top. With the beds set up, she says she won't till the beds again. To maintain the beds she adds mulch and organic matter to the surface each spring and fall. Her soil looks beautiful, and so do her vegetables.

Carolyn and Earl Lawrence have a hard clay soil on their southern Virginia farm. Through chisel plowing, surface disking, manuring, cover cropping, green manuring, and a strict crop rotation they have developed it into a viable organic vegetable farm.

Of special interest to us was that with little work and no tilling they were able to produce a soil in their kitchen garden as good or better than that in their commercial farm. Furthermore, they estimate that the soil improvement accomplished in a single growing season in the kitchen garden is comparable to three to five years' work on the farm soil.

To do this the Lawrences lay baled hay, solidly, one bale deep across their new garden area (see Figure 111). They then spread five- or six-inch-deep strips of compost across the top of the bales and plant their seeds directly in these compost strips. The vegetables grow prolifically atop the bales, which decompose down to a depth of 2½ to 3 inches over their growing season (see Figure 112). The Lawrences have an ample supply of hay bales on their farm, since the price of hay falls so low in some years that they choose to return the hay to the soil rather than sell it at no profit. This practice makes sense for their kitchen garden, though it would not be appropriate, nor would they have an adequate supply of hay, on the farm scale. Obviously, many people won't have the quantity of hay bales necessary to cover their whole garden, but in difficult soil conditions it could be tried on individual garden beds.

The Lawrence family is trying a similar technique in a smaller area which their son plans to

**Figure 110** *Janney Munsell in her garden in Maine.*

**Figure 111** *Earl and Carolyn Lawrence create a garden area on their hard clay earth in Virginia by spreading baled hay solidly across the area, one bale deep.*

PHOTO BY TIMOTHY FISHER.

PHOTO BY TIMOTHY FISHER.

**Figure 112** *After only one year, the baled hay in the Lawrence's garden decomposed to form this black humus, which is scraped aside in this photo to show the clay underneath.*

use for tulip propagation. One course of hay bales has been laid around the new garden space, forming a low wall, and the enclosed area is filled with compost materials that break down into a rich growing medium.

## MOUND GARDENING

Another interesting minimum-till soil-building technique is mound gardening. We have not had a chance to try it yet ourselves, nor could we locate practitioners of the method in this country. But based on the German booklet (available in En-glish) *Mound Cultivation,*[7] it seems to achieve through different means the same goals of other intensive soil preparation methods.

Constructed similarly to a compost pile, the mound garden beds support growing vegetables during the decomposition process. The plants benefit from the warmth of decomposition, as in a hotbed, and the bed provides a rich garden soil. Since the mound is built of such coarse organic

[7] Hans Beba and Hermann Andrä. *Mound Cultivation.* Translated from the German, *Hügelkultur,* by Karen and Duncan Horne (Mannheim, West Germany: Waerland-Verlag, 1979).

75

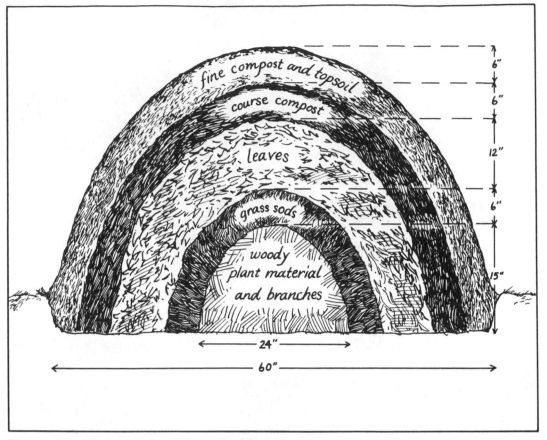

**Figure 113**  *The construction of a mound garden bed.*

matter as fruit tree prunings and the like, and also because it is not disturbed, the decomposition process produces a much milder heat than a hot-bed, and is reported to continue for five or six years.

Each mound is a long berm about 5 feet wide at its base and 3 or 4 feet tall at the time of its construction, though it sinks as the plant materials decompose (see Figure 113). A shallow trench is dug out for the area of the new mound, and the sods are removed in squares and saved. A 24-inch-wide and 15-inch-high core of small branches cut in short pieces is laid down the middle of this trench, and the sod that was removed is placed grass side down on top of the branches. Atop the sod goes 12 inches of leaves weighted down with a few spadefuls of soil. Next comes a layer of a couple inches of well-rotted manure, followed by several inches of moist peat. The entire mound is topped with a mixture of compost, peat, and topsoil raked evenly and patted down to hold its form. During the five or six years which the mound gradually sinks and decomposes the gardener need do nothing for the mound beyond the occasional topdressing of compost and organic matter. After

the sixth year one is no longer receiving the low heat of the decomposition process, though a rich garden compost remains.

## WET SOILS

If your garden is too wet, your soil preparation may correct the problem. Often the addition of organic matter and sand may be all that is necessary. One Vermont gardener, in a wet location where water saturated his beds late into the spring, found it advantageous to do his basic bed preparation in the fall. He rakes each bed up into a rough-surfaced peaked ridge to shed water and leaves it that way through the winter. In the spring he rakes the bed flat, and it is ready to plant.

Poor drainage on a clay soil was the primary reason that Winnie Amato, of Medina, Ohio, chose to establish her raised bed garden. Her combination of raised beds and trenched paths has eliminated her drainage problems. In fact, she has turned her clay into such a rich wormy soil that she has won first prize for her vegetables at the county fair.

To prepare her garden Winnie Amato tilled the entire area and laid out 4-foot by 4-foot wooden frames about 8 inches high on the tilled area. She allowed for paths about 2 feet wide between the beds. The path areas were dug into trenches, depositing the soil from the trenches into the boxed beds, and the trenches were filled with corncobs, a waste product in her corn-growing area. Lawn cuttings are also added to the paths as the season progresses. The corncob-filled trenches act as a drainage area for the beds, eventually decomposing into a humus. The clay in the garden is mixed with sand, compost, and chicken manure to make a healthy loam. With her beds established, Winnie points out that she no longer rototills the garden and is able to work the garden earlier in the spring.

The conventional agricultural soil drainage method is either ditching or installing a buried drain tile network carrying excess water to lower ground. This is rather expensive and time-consuming, but it is effective and should be considered where simpler methods don't work.

## EROSION

Erosion is a serious concern to any gardener trying to build a rich soil and to any citizen who recognizes the necessity of maintaining soil fertility for the survival of future generations.

In parts of the world with hillside agricultural traditions, such as the Mediterranean, much of Asia, and the Andes, permanent stone wall terracing is a standard erosion control without which agriculture could not have survived (see Figure 114). In severe terrain the example of these cultures is well worth following. In addition to stone, retaining walls can be made of planks, railroad ties, logs, concrete blocks and bricks, or they can be an earthen berm maintained in a permanent ground cover.

**Figure 114** *Terracing is common in places with a hillside agricultural tradition. In these terraced beds in southern Italy, citrus trees are covered with a protective netting.*

PHOTO BY TIMOTHY FISHER.

**Figure 115** *Tony Bok's terraced beds in Maine.*

The intensive gardener has the option of either terracing a large garden area or terracing each bed individually. Even on moderate slopes your garden beds should follow the contour of the land, each bed acting as a dam preventing precious soil from washing down the hill.

In order to counter erosion on his "Hillside Farm" in Maine, Tony Bok has adopted a system of terraced beds stretching across the steep slope of his commercial vegetable garden (see Figure 115). To establish the beds he rototilled the garden area and marked out 4-foot-wide beds with 2-foot-wide paths. He rakes the dirt uphill out of each path, building up the low side of the bed above until it is level. He always rakes uphill to counter the effect of soil washed down the hill through erosion.

Ray Nelson of nearby Friendship, Maine, has also established terraced beds along the contours of his hillside garden (see Figure 116). He has refined this method by keeping his paths planted in a permanent sod to assist further in controlling erosion. He mulches extensively for the same reason. As he says, "I try to do as little damage to the natural world as I can, and do as nature does. Nature doesn't leave soil bare." Ray also lays rocks along the lower edge of the beds to stabilize them.

Cover crops and mulching are valuable practices, which, among their other benefits, help to hold the soil in garden beds. Cover crops can be seeded just before or after a bed is harvested. Mulches are useful both during and after the growing season.

**Figure 116** *Ray Nelson contours his beds across the hillside and leaves his paths in a permanent sod to control erosion.*

## PATHS

The treatment of paths between garden beds is important to most gardeners even where erosion is not a problem. Most people garden for pleasure in addition to food. A muddy or hard and dry path is not pleasant to work on (see Figure 117). Permanent grass and/or legume paths are attractive, pleasant to work on, and hold the soil. As always, legumes may improve the soil in which they are grown as well as provide the other benefits of a ground cover. However, sod paths must be mown regularly, and, particularly with unboxed-in beds, the edges of the paths must be maintained to prevent them from encroaching into the beds.

Sheet composting and mulches are also satisfactory path treatments. With unboxed beds many gardeners like to mulch the sloping sides of the beds in addition to the paths. Common mulching materials are hay, grass clippings, leaves, wood-chips, etc. (see Figure 118). Newspaper is often used as a mulch, but it is usually held down by another mulch material to keep it from blowing away. Organic mulches must be replenished frequently because they decompose and weeds begin to grow through them, but, of course, all that rotted mulch is enriching the garden soil.

More permanent paths can be made of paving materials such as concrete, brick, or stone. These materials will also absorb solar heat during the day, radiating that stored heat to the surrounding soil and air at night.

Weeds growing in the paths are not necessarily a bad thing. After all, some weeds are an effective ground cover. Just because they are self-sowing does not make them undesirable. One North Carolina gardener told us, "In the spring we eat

**Figure 118** *A garden path mulched with wood chips in Janney and David Munsell's Maine garden.*

out of the paths." She said many of the edible weeds growing wild in the paths, such as amaranth, chickweed, dandelions, sourgrass, and purslane, were a large part of their diet in the early spring before they had many vegetables. But path weeds can get out of control if their roots encroach into the beds. If they are not kept cut, the weeds go to seed, sowing more weeds in the beds, where they may overwhelm, or at least retard, the domesticated vegetables. Many weeds not only spread their seeds, but creep and spread by root division. Eventually, even edible weeds like purslane and sheep sorrel can become a major nuisance if not rooted out.

## TRANSPLANTING AND SUCCESSIONS

The planning chapter discusses why it is desirable to use transplants in an intensive garden and how to grow them. After all the work of growing them, take the necessary care to plant them well. Handle the transplants carefully, making sure not to damage the roots as you take them from their contain-

**Figure 117** *A muddy path is not pleasant to work in.*

79

ers. Peat pots, or their paper equivalent, which you can plant without having to disturb the young plants, will make this easier. Transplanting is best done in late afternoon in order that the plants will have the cool and dark of night to adapt to their new environment before facing the hot sun. Depending on conditions, you may want to construct simple shields of paper or mulch around new transplants to protect them from the sun or wind when they are first set out. Always water seedlings promptly upon transplanting, and give them special attention until they become established.

## FERTILIZING DURING THE GROWING SEASON

Most intensive gardeners rely upon a rich soil preparation to provide the nutrients needed by their vegetables. In addition to the fertilizer added to the soil in the digging process, many gardeners, prior to seeding or transplanting, use a top dressing of compost or liquid fertilizer during the growing period. Your bed preparation provides a generalized, longer-term fertility throughout the bed, and liquid fertilizers can be applied to a specific

plant or area for its immediate use. Common liquid fertilizers are fish emulsion, urine, or a slurry made of water and manure called manure tea. All the liquid fertilizers are usually applied with lots of water to insure that they penetrate through surface soil down to the plant roots. A fertilizer such as liquid seaweed is used by some gardeners as a foliar spray. The liquid seaweed is sprayed directly on the plants' leaves, where the nutrients are absorbed by the plant, giving it a quick spurt. When using commercial preparations of these liquids, be sure to use them in strengths not exceeding those recommended on the labels.

## USING MULCHES IN BEDS

Mulches have already been discussed in terms of path treatment. The idea of a living mulch created by growing plants themselves that shade out weeds and retain moisture is covered in Chapter 3. We will discuss here mulches used within the growing area. This mulch can be either organic, such as hay, woodchips, seaweed, or leaves, or inert, such as plastic, tin, or rocks (see Figures 119–121). Each has its advantages and disadvantages, but each is

**Figure 119** *Hay used as mulch in Paul and Debbie Doscher's New Hampshire garden.*

PHOTO BY TIMOTHY FISHER.

**Figure 120** *Grass used as mulch in the garden of Norman and Sherrie Lee in New York.*

PHOTO BY TIMOTHY FISHER.

used to cover the soil around vegetables to prevent weed growth and retain soil moisture.

The nicest feature of an organic mulch is that by decomposing it adds organic matter and nutrients to the soil. On the other hand, because it decomposes, you must replenish the mulch or it ceases to be an effective weed control. Mulch, particularly hay, can also introduce weed seeds into your garden. One gardener told us that because of weed seeds in hay he now leaves it outside for a year to rot before using it: "When it's slimy and black, it's ready to go."

A thick layer of mulch acts to insulate the soil from the extremes of air temperature. This can be beneficial in midsummer to keep the soil from baking, or as a moderator between day and night temperatures through the growing season. But a thick mulch, because it prevents the soil from warming up, can also retard a vegetable's growth in the spring, particularly in the northern regions. In this situation it is better not to mulch until later in the season (usually midsummer), when the soil has warmed.

A black plastic polyethylene covering for vegetable beds is popular with both commercial and home gardeners (see Figure 122). After the bed has been prepared, but before planting, the polyethyl-

**Figure 122** *A black polyethylene mulch used on raised beds on the vegetable farm of Howard Prusack in Vermont.*

ene is rolled down the length of the bed. It can be held in place with a few shovelfuls of earth on the edges or nails driven through the plastic into the soil, or, for a more rustic appearance, the edges of the plastic covered with woodchips. The gardener then cuts a slit in the plastic and inserts a transplant through the slit into the soil. To plant from seed, slightly larger holes should be made in the plastic. The plant growing through the plastic suffers no competition from weeds, and the black color acts to warm the soil in the beds. This heat can be an advantage or disadvantage, depending on the crops being grown. Unless one is careful to create bowl depressions around each plant, much of the rainwater will wash off the bed, but the plastic also acts as a moisture barrier preventing moisture from escaping from the bed.

Many gardeners object to polyethylene on aesthetic grounds, or because it contributes nothing to the soil as does an organic mulch. Though some gardeners are able to get several years' use out of a sheet of polyethylene, it does deteriorate with age, leaving some pieces of this inorganic material in the soil. Additionally, we question the environmental soundness of using nonrenewable petrochemicals to create a mulching material of such limited durability. Some sheet plastic mulches are available with a longer life expectancy than polyethylene, but they are also more expensive. Salvaged steel roofing with holes cut out for plants to

**Figure 121** *Newspaper mulch in the garden of Heather and Don Parker in Maine.*

**Figure 123** *Stone mulches absorb the sun's heat during the day, keeping the soil warmer through the night. Garden at the Rodale Old Farm in Pennsylvania.*

grow can be used to the same effect as plastic sheeting and should be reusable for many years.

Stone mulches are another possibility (see Figure 123). The stones, like other mulches, displace weeds and retain moisture. Their big advantage is that the rocks absorb the sun's heat during the day, keeping the soil warmer through the night. Jeff Moyer at the Rodale Experimental Farm in Emmaus, Pennsylvania, told us that their stone-mulched area makes the soil warmer by a couple of degrees, extending their season in both spring and fall. The disadvantage with stone mulches is they are a lot of work to establish, and, once established, are relatively permanent, limiting your alternatives. There is also a considerable weeding problem between the stones. Concrete slabs or bricks would lessen the weed problem. If you can obtain surplus or broken roofing or floor slate, you can make a more easily movable rock mulch, in which the square cut pieces fit together well, lessening the problem of weeds.

Boards can also be used as a mulch between plants. They will eventually decompose, though not in a single growing season. A problem with boards, though, is that unless they are well sealed or painted, they will warp, because they are exposed to the sun's warmth on one side and the soil's moisture on the other. As this makes them curl up at the edges, they become less effective at preventing weed growth.

Old car tires are very popular mulches around large warmth-loving vegetables like tomatoes and eggplant. In addition to mulching, the tires give some wind protection to the young plants and absorb the sun's heat (see Figure 124). Often the inside of the tire is filled with stones to store this heat. The tire interior can be filled with rich soil, making a mini-raised bed.

## WEEDS

Weed control is an integral part of intensive gardening. By using transplants, establishing a living mulch, using mulches, and with careful bed preparation, weeds should be much less of a problem than in a conventional garden. What weeds spring up are easy to pull from the loose soil in the beds. Some gardeners use a tiller whenever possible between crops to cut down weeds, whereas other gardeners think that a rototiller only turns up dormant weed seeds, which proceed to sprout in the garden. It is worthwhile to keep weeds in areas surrounding your beds mowed to prevent them from going to seed and sowing themselves in your beds. Winter mulches and cover crops should

**Figure 124** *Tires absorb the sun's heat, making them a good mulch for these heat loving tomatoes. Garden of Sam and Elizabeth Smith in Massachusetts.*

lessen the number of weeds in garden beds in the spring, though cover crops, if allowed to go to seed, can themselves become a nuisance.

Finally, though weeds cannot be allowed to dominate the vegetables, a few weeds do no harm; they can serve as a living mulch until vegetables grow large enough to fill that role. If a garden is abandoned or ignored, weeds establish themselves quickly to conserve the precious soil.

It is important to distinguish between weeds that are a problem and those that are not. Weeds like lamb's-quarters and wild mustard reproduce from seed and hence can be brought under control by mowing and minimizing surface cultivation. When these weeds do sprout, they are relatively easy to uproot in the characteristic loose soil of the intensive garden. There are other weeds, however, that are not so easily dealt with. Weeds such as witch grass and milkweed, which proliferate from the roots or have very deep roots or rhizomes, can be a real nuisance. The best thing to do is to learn to recognize these plants and pick out the vital roots, runners, or rhizomes while digging the bed. Time spent doing this is well repaid when it comes to weeding, because tough grasses that are firmly locked into a deep underground root system will be nearly impossible to pull out effectively. In dealing with these problem weeds a rototiller may multiply the problem by chopping and distributing the living roots.

## Pests

Pests are inevitable in a garden sooner or later. We tend to take a somewhat philosophical view toward this. As one gardener we visited claims: "If a vegetable isn't good enough for a bug, it isn't good enough for me." As far as insect pests go, the health of your plants is your best defense. A certain percentage of chewed and sucked leaves or flowers are normal to any garden, and do little harm. They should not be considered a problem unless yields are considerably lessened because of it.

A species living upon an alien organism as a parasite only develops into a disease organism of the host when its component individuals grow so numerous and active that the latter is debilitated. But there are in nature numerous examples of parasitism in which the vigour of the host is such that it is able to support the parasite without impairing its own health. . . .

True parasites, however indifferent to the host, are always potential disease organisms, and their relative harmlessness, in certain conditions, is a function, not of their own nature, but of the surplus energy and power of the host.[8]

Understanding this ecological principle may not solve your immediate problem, but we think it's a good reflection of the extent to which man ought (or ought not) to exert his control in this area. It is backed up by many gardeners we have talked to, who plant a little more than they need and expect to lose some plants. Still, this is no comfort when you find an unreasonable onslaught of pesky eaters in your garden. It happens to every gardener at one time or another. Don't overlook sanitation and quarantine as tools to defeat diseases or pests. Clean up dead or dying vegetation and destroy it. Try not to handle the affected plants, and, if you do, don't handle other susceptible plants afterward.

There are pesticides and biological controls that many organic gardeners feel free to use. Rotenone, pyrethrum, and *Bacillus thuringiensis* are widely used among gardeners with whom we have discussed the matter. These are perhaps the easiest and most convenient solutions, since you can have them on hand and use them if and when a problem develops. Rotenone and pyrethrum, derived from plants, have short-term effects and are of low toxicity to man and animals. They both come in powders and can be used as is or made into a solution with water and used as a spray. Pyrethrum is the less toxic and, to be effective, must be sprayed or dusted directly on the insects. The drawback of these two substances that gardeners most often note is that they are not specific—that is, they are harmful to many insects. This brings us to an important point in the business of insect pests in the garden. Of all the many insects that live in your garden only a very small number are likely to cause you trouble. Many of them, in fact, benefit your plants. Consequently, many gardeners sensi-

[8] Edward Hyams. *Soil and Civilization* (New York: Harper and Row, 1976), p. 28.

bly feel that the damage done by a few species of bugs is more than offset by the help the plants receive from many other insects, and they leave well enough alone.

*Bacillus thuringiensis* is a bacteria that attacks the intestines of soft-bodied worms; unlike rotenone and pyrethrum, it is specific to this type of insect. It is used mostly to kill cabbage worms and loopers. Milky spore disease, *Bacillus popilliae,* is another bacteria and is used to control Japanese beetles.

Another technique people use to control problem insects is picking them off by hand. This is a tedious business and can be recommended only for large insects like potato bugs. Some people also use a high-pressure water spray to dislodge harmful insects like aphids and whiteflies. In the case of cutworms, which kill young plants by chomping through their stems, it may be a good idea to have a number of refill plants ready to transplant into the vacated space. Be sure to kill the cutworm, which is hiding just under the soil surface near its victim, before putting in a replacement. Cutworm damage can often be prevented by shielding transplants with a collar pressed into the soil. This can be of paper, cardboard, or metal, and should be an inch or two in diameter and 3 to 4 inches tall, pressed 1 inch into the soil (see Figure 125).

Encouraging predators in your garden is helpful control. Some people keep guinea fowl or quail in the garden to consume excessive insect populations. Attracting birds to your garden in general is

**Figure 125** *A collar to protect young transplants from cutworms.*

an easy way to keep the insect community in check, though you may have some problems with birds eating seeds. Birdhouses and feeders, hedges, and berry bushes will invite birds into your garden. Encouraging predatory insects in the garden is another aid. This may be as casual as transferring every ladybug you come across to your aphid-infested plants. It may, on the other hand, mean buying a quantity of ladybugs to release in your garden. In many areas, unfortunately for the gardener, ladybugs released in this way may fly away. Praying mantises will consume a fair share of insects, including aphids, caterpillars, and grasshoppers.

Traps are also used to exterminate difficult insects. We have seen a number of gardeners use a dish of beer or a board lying around in the garden to attract slugs, which are subsequently drowned or killed. Many gardeners sport purchased Japanese beetle traps.

Animals, too, can do a lot of illicit nibbling in your garden. When this occurs, the first thing to do is check your fences, and mend or reinforce them if necessary. Of course, a fence is not foolproof, not when it takes one 12 feet high to discourage deer. A dog in your garden can inhibit the activities of four-legged vegetarians. A light at night may work too, or some kind of noisemaker. Often, though, these are short-term deterrents, as the offending animals readily adapt and become accustomed to the light and noise. Dried blood was used by some gardeners we've talked to, sprinkled around the area under attack. Another idea suggested by a gardener is loose chicken wire laid horizontally in its characteristic lumpy furls along the ground to entangle raccoons attempting a garden raid.

We have not gone into this subject in much depth, for many other books offer a better resource on this subject than we can expect to offer here. However, when the desperation of vegetable loss looms before you, there are ideas here that will be able to help. In any case, take heart. Our own experience, backed by that of other people, seems to show that your pest problems are most likely to occur within the first few years after you establish your garden. This is because making a garden upsets the previous natural balance, and it takes time to adjust and establish a new balance suited to your garden.

## PREPARATION FOR WINTER

As the summer growing season ends and harvesting is done, there still remains some work for the gardener. The garden needs to be cleaned up for the winter and made ready for the next spring. Stakes, trellises, and solar intensive devices not being used over the winter must be put away. Any diseased plants should be burned to prevent the overwintering of the disease. The remaining annual plants should be composted or sheet-composted. If you use cover crops, they should be planted in time for the cover crop to become established before the weather turns too cold for further growth. If not, a winter mulch will be a good practice to prevent erosion over the winter. Any plants you intend to leave in your garden over the winter will benefit from a mulch cover.

## PREPARATION FOR NEXT SPRING

A considerable amount of your next year's gardening can be done the previous fall. Some gardeners do the majority of their bed preparation in the fall and can proceed directly with planting in the spring. Where there is a deep snow cover until near planting time, this can be a great advantage in allowing you to take the best advantage of a short growing season. Similarly, if you set out solar intensive devices in the very early spring or have left them through the winter, you may have had to shovel snow away to find the bed. You will be grateful to have the bed all prepared for early planting. (Instead of shoveling to remove snow, wood ashes sprinkled on the snow cause the sun to melt that area much faster than the surrounding snow.)

Fall sowing is another way to get a headstart on spring. We have often had peas, lettuce, and spinach come up on their own in our garden, self-seeded from the previous year. And usually these seedlings, regulated by their own calendars, have a considerable headstart over the seeds of the same species planted in the spring. By purposefully planting these seeds in the fall, you can benefit from early plants, planted where you want them to be, even if you are too occupied with other spring projects to get the rest of your seed in on time.

You can also plant semihardy plants (such as the Brassicas) toward the end of the summer growing season, and they will grow only a little through the fall. When it gets too cold for their continued growth, they should be covered with a thick mulch to protect them through the winter. Come spring, these plants, well established the previous fall, will grow quickly, not having to wait for warm weather to germinate, nor suffering the shock of transplanting.

# 5

## SOLAR INTENSIVE COLD-SEASON GARDENING

Paul Doscher

WE HAVE all experienced it. The last of the winter snow is almost gone except in the most sheltered corners of the yard. The sun is getting higher in the sky every day, and the early wildflowers are beginning to appear. A few days each week the temperature rises into the 60's and 70's. The temptation to get out and plant the garden is almost irresistible, yet you know that it will still be another month or two before the danger of frost is past. In New Hampshire this itch inevitably hits before the end of March (last frost date averages around May 20), yet for most gardeners the only way to satisfy it is to plant flats of tomatoes, peppers, eggplants, and cabbage on a sunny windowsill. Going out into the garden to plant lettuce, radishes, and cabbage is considered a bit foolish (though it is all right to plant peas) and the idea of harvesting greens for a fresh salad is simply ridiculous.

In our solar intensive garden these old ideas are forgotten. The only season when something cannot be grown, harvested, or planted is the two-month period from mid-December to early February. Cold hardy greens are started early in two de-

vices called solar hot frames and Solar Pods (see Figure 126). The hot frame is similar to the traditional cold frame, but is fully insulated to keep out winter cold and hold in solar heat. The Pod is a device that is installed over a permanent bed, framed with wood and rigid insulation, and is a double-glazed cover with a unique curved profile. In mid-spring still more plants are transplanted into the garden under our twentieth-century versions of the cloches used by the traditional Parisian market gardeners. Then, in early summer, when cool nights still come quite frequently, heat-loving crops like melons and cucumbers are set out to thrive under cold frames or Pods. While neighbors are wondering why their melons are "just sitting there doing nothing," ours are growing inches each day, and the first flowers are beginning to bloom.

As the summer progresses, we continue to plant. Our late summer seedlings will become our fall and winter crops. When the first frost hits (usually around September 5) our fall crops of lettuce, carrots, cabbage, broccoli, kale, chard, and other vegetables are under cover of cold frames, cloches, or in

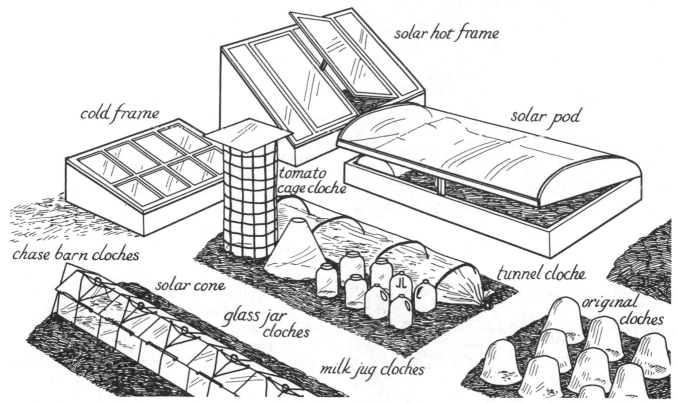

**Figure 126** *There are a variety of solar intensive devices both old and new which can be used to extend the intensive garden season.*

our solar hot frame. Salads with fresh tomatoes, peppers, and cucumbers continue a month or so beyond the first frost, from plants that have been protected on the coldest nights.

When the 10°F nights of December arrive, the lettuce in our Pods is dealt a fatal blow. But in the solar hot frame Swiss chard, radishes, leaf lettuce, Chinese cabbage, beets, and parsley still keep growing, slowly but surely. Only the subzero temperatures of January put a temporary halt to our bountiful harvest from the solar frame. The plants will survive the winter, though, and begin to grow again in late February, with harvesting starting again in March.

Our solar intensive garden has made it possible for us to have fresh vegetables almost year round. The methods we use are simple and relatively inexpensive, and in moderate climates can provide harvests during all twelve months of the year. With some planning, some thought, some skill in carpentry and horticulture, and a touch of enthusiasm, you can do the same.

## THE SOLAR INTENSIVE GARDEN IN SPRING

All good gardens begin with planning and preparation. Since you will want to get into your solar intensive garden early in the spring, perhaps even in late winter, your preparations should be completed during the previous fall and winter. Preparation involves six steps:

1. Site selection
2. Construction of beds, including permanent, insulated beds and solar devices to cover them
3. Soil preparation in the fall
4. Crop selection
5. Soil finishing and possibly manure bed preparation in spring
6. Starting of seedlings indoors or in a greenhouse for transplanting into the garden

The first three steps must be accomplished the previous fall, before the ground freezes. The last three steps are good activities for the cold days of

**Figure 127** *Springtime bed preparation in Leandre and Gretchen Poisson's garden in New Hampshire.*

**Figure 128** *The Poisson's garden in summer.*

**Figure 129** *January in the Poisson's garden.*

winter and early spring. Once you have them all completed, you will be on your way to producing amazingly early crops (see Figures 127–129).

## SITE SELECTION

As we mentioned in Chapter 3, you should select a spot for your solar intensive beds which is well drained, receives full sun all day through the fall and late winter, and is close enough to your house to provide convenient access for your daily gardening chores. Having water close by is also helpful.

## SOLAR INTENSIVE DEVICES

There are many systems and items to choose from. They range from the very simple, milk-jug cloche and fiberglass cone to uninsulated cold frames or lights, to insulated permanent beds covered by double-glazed Pods. Beyond all these there is the fully insulated solar hot frame, which is a hybrid between the cold frame and a solar greenhouse. Most of the devices can be built by the user, and many can be purchased in local garden stores or through specialized mail order catalogs. We describe them in detail in Chapter 6.

You can begin your planting about three to four weeks earlier than normal if you use lightweight portable cloches. The original glass cloches were heavy and very fragile, but many of the materials you can use to construct modern cloches are durable, lightweight, and inexpensive. Cloches are used in your regular garden beds to provide a warm miniclimate for starting a wide variety of greens and root crops. They can also be used to protect early plantings of frost-sensitive plants like tomatoes, peppers, eggplants, melons, etc. Individual cloches, such as cut off milk jugs and food jars, are inexpensive or free, and should be easy to obtain. The fiberglass cone is simple to construct, is very durable, and can be made in almost any size you want. Continuous cloches made of glass, plastic, or polyethylene and wire are becoming more common. Continuous cloches made of glass once covered acres of land in Europe, and were used to produce extra early harvests of lettuce, cauliflower, strawberries, and many other crops (see Figure 130).

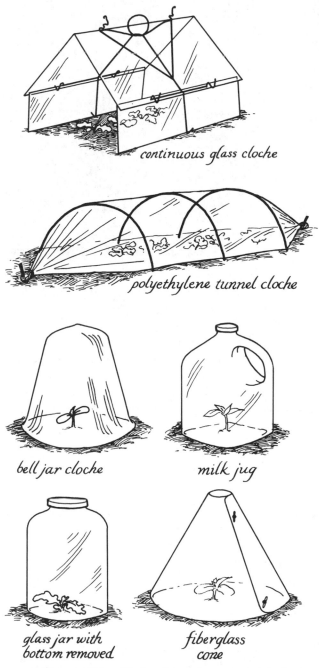

*continuous glass cloche*

*polyethylene tunnel cloche*

*bell jar cloche*　　*milk jug*

*glass jar with bottom removed*　　*fiberglass cone*

**Figure 130**　*Cloches for getting a few weeks jump on the growing season.*

harden off seedlings that are to be set out after danger of frost is past (see Figure 131).

Cold frames are best oriented east to west, and are lower in height on the south side. The angle of the glass allows the frame to catch the low winter sun.

Cold frames or lights can also be used to cover manure hotbeds. ("Lights" is a term used to describe the cold-frame sash used by European market gardeners.) Lights are similar to cold frames, differing in that they are completely portable and are used in large numbers to cover entire beds (see Figure 27). When these devices are used to cover manure-heated beds, plants benefit not only from the heat of the air provided by the sun, but from the bottom heating of the soil.

An equally early start can be achieved using an insulated cold frame or the Solar Pod. Construction involves building a permanent wooden or masonry base in the ground. The base is insulated down into the ground to conserve soil heat. Each base is designed to accommodate one glazed cover. The size of the homemade insulated cold frame is usually determined by the size of the window to be used as a cover.

Pods, however, are a standard 4 by 8 feet and are oriented with the long dimension running north and south. The cover has a curved surface; this allows the sun to shine into the bed all day long. Pods are often double glazed, which holds in

**Figure 131**　*A low cost, portable cold frame constructed with an old storm window.*

PHOTO BY PAUL DOSCHER.

If you are content to start your gardening a month or month and a half before normal, you can use an uninsulated cold frame. Most gardeners have seen or used one, and its advantages are low cost and portability. It can be used to grow early crops in the garden or in the traditional fashion, to

**Figure 132**  *An insulated Solar Pod.*

**Figure 133**  *A Pod in the spring.*

more nighttime heat than a single glazed cover (see Figures 132–133).

If you want the earliest spring start, you should choose the solar hot frame idea. This device is both a permanent bed and cover all in one (see Figures 134–135). It is insulated above and below the ground to hold soil heat and warm air. It may also have an insulated shutter, which significantly reduces nighttime heat loss through the glazed cover. In New England it is possible to get plants started in the device in late February or early March, when the snow is still a foot or two deep outdoors.

You should decide in the fall which devices you want to use. This will give you plenty of time to build permanent beds and covers before the snow falls. Simple cloches can be built at any time, but frames for permanent beds should be in the ground before it freezes for the winter. If you keep your permanent beds covered all winter, the soil in the beds will not freeze (or not very deeply), and this will give you an earlier start in the spring. Be sure to provide some support or protection for your glass and fiberglass covers. Heavy winter snow may damage them or otherwise break them.

## SOIL PREPARATION IN THE FALL

If you have built a good garden soil for your summer intensive garden, you will be able to use the same soil for your solar intensive beds. If your soil is still not as well prepared as it should be, you can

**Figure 134**  *An insulated solar hot frame that incorporates an insulated thermal shutter for keeping heat in at night.*

**Figure 135**  *The Doscher's solar frame in early spring.*

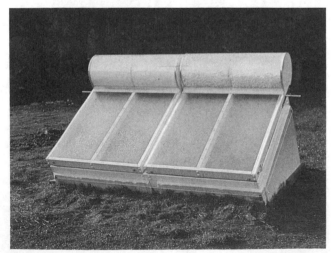

make an acceptable mixture by combining two parts of your loam or clay with one part coarse sand and one part well-decomposed organic matter. For organic matter you can use peat moss, compost, leaf mold, or well-rotted manure.

The soil should be prepared during the fall and allowed to sit undisturbed for the winter, unless it is to be used for fall crops. If fall crops are grown, prepare the soil after they are harvested. Fertilizing can be done at this time, but you should be conservative in your use of fresh organic matter.

## SOIL FINISHING IN SPRING

In late winter you should work the soil as soon as possible, then check for nutrient and pH levels. At this time it should not be necessary to add organic matter, since that was done in the fall.

Next, you should prepare a seed or transplant bed as you would normally do. After this you must prewarm the soil. This is done by placing the cloches in the locations where you will have seedlings, or, with cold frames and Pods, by keeping the covers closed and free of snow and ice. You will be able to plant earliest in insulated devices, and latest under cloches. As a rule of thumb, you should wait until soil temperature has warmed up to 60° F or higher during the day and not less than 45° F at night. Measure the temperature at a depth of 1 to 3 inches (see Figure 136).

**Figure 136** *A soil thermometer is an essential tool for the solar intensive gardener. Before planting be sure that the soil temperatures are high enough to allow for good germination.*

## SOIL TEMPERATURES FOR BEST SEED GERMINATION

| Crop | Minimum F° | Optimum Range (°F) | Maximum °F |
|---|---|---|---|
| Asparagus | 50 | 60–85 | 95 |
| Beans, lima | 60 | 65–85 | 85 |
| Beans, snap | 60 | 60–85 | 95 |
| Beets | 40 | 50–85 | 95 |
| Cabbage | 40 | 45–95 | 100 |
| Carrots | 40 | 45–85 | 95 |
| Cauliflower | 40 | 45–85 | 100 |
| Celery | 40 | 60–70 | 85* |
| Corn | 50 | 60–95 | 105 |
| Cucumbers | 60 | 65–90 | 105 |
| Eggplant | 60 | 75–90 | 95 |
| Lettuce | 35 | 40–80 | 85 |
| Muskmelon | 60 | 75–95 | 100 |
| Okra | 60 | 70–95 | 105 |
| Onions | 35 | 50–95 | 95 |
| Parsley | 40 | 50–85 | 90 |
| Parsnips | 35 | 50–70 | 85 |
| Peas | 40 | 40–75 | 85 |
| Peppers | 60 | 65–95 | 95 |
| Pumpkin | 60 | 70–90 | 100 |
| Radish | 40 | 45–90 | 95 |
| Swiss chard | 40 | 50–85 | 95 |
| Spinach | 35 | 45–75 | 85 |
| Squash | 60 | 70–95 | 100 |
| Tomatoes | 50 | 60–85 | 95 |
| Turnips | 40 | 60–105 | 105 |
| Watermelon | 60 | 70–95 | 105 |

\* Nighttime temperature must drop to 60°F or lower for good germination.

Compiled by J. F. Harrington, Department of Vegetable Crops, University of California at Davis.

It is difficult to give specific dates for doing any of this. In New Hampshire there is actually enough sun in late February to transplant some cold hardy crops into insulated Pods and hot frames. However, it is not possible to direct seed into the Pods until the soil warms up in mid-March. In other locations these dates will vary considerably. The best way to judge your own climate is to take regular air and soil temperature readings inside the solar intensive device you are using with a minimum-maximum thermometer and soil thermometer. The first spring you may not pick the best planting times, but after a couple of years of experience you will know when to select planting and transplanting dates for your area.

## MANURE HEATING

In the past French intensive gardeners used large quantities of fermenting manure to provide warm soil for early spring planting. This method works best in spring, because the heat given off by the manure is hottest just after the beds are prepared and gradually drops off as the season progresses. Correspondingly, the spring weather begins to warm up as the manure cools down, providing the possibility of creating an optimal growing environment from planting to harvest.

If you choose to try using manure hotbeds, use the following method as your guide (and refer to Figure 137):

1. Excavate the area you will be using to about 2 to 2½ feet deep. If you are building your hotbed in an insulated, permanent bed, the size of your excavation is limited by the size of the bed frame. If you are going to use portable frames and lights like those used by the French, the excavation should extend at least 6 to 12 inches wider than the frame of the light. Your trench should be deeper on heavy, wet soil than on warm, sandy soil.
2. Obtain fresh horse manure that contains lots of bedding. Straw bedding is preferable to sawdust. Pile your manure near the garden and turn it at least once to get it to start heating up. You may want to measure the temperature in the pile to determine when it has dropped down to about 100°F to 120°F. Do not use it fresh, because in the early stages of decomposition some manures can reach 140°F to 160°F, and this is too hot for plants.
3. If you want to provide a more constant, lower heat, you should mix your manure with leaves, hay, or rotted manure. Some early books on the subject recommended using a 50/50 combination of fresh and rotted material.
4. After the temperature of the fermenting manure has begun to drop, shovel it into the pit in layers a few inches deep. Get in there and tread down each layer with your feet until it is well compressed. Fill the bed until you are within about 6 inches of the top.
5. Water the manure all over so that it is moist (but not soaked) throughout.
6. Next you can add a layer of straw about 2 inches thick. This will help reduce the immediate impact of the heat upon plant roots by providing a small amount of insulation. This is not absolutely necessary, however.
7. Now add a 6-inch layer of loose rich topsoil over the entire bed.
8. Center your cold frame or light frame over the bed. Allow a day or two for the manure to start working again and for the soil to warm up before planting. Be sure the temperature in the top few inches of soil is no higher than about 75°F. If the temperature is higher than this, you may have to wait a few more days before planting seeds or transplants. It is best to use transplants, since the warm moist environment in the frame can be conducive to seed rotting or damping-off fungus. Be sure to select healthy transplants large enough to be unaffected by the fungus.

As an alternative to using manure for heating, you can use electric heating units like soil-warming cables. They can be used in many applications and in both permanent and regular beds. However, we try to stay away from using such devices, as they greatly increase the nonsolar energy input into the garden and can be quite expensive to operate.

## CROP SELECTION

Your choice of spring crops for the solar intensive garden is somewhat limited compared with your summer selection. The difference comes in the need to use crops that grow well under the cooler conditions prevalent in the early spring. If you will be planting directly into your beds using seeds, you will have also to choose seeds that germinate well under cool soil conditions. Of course, if you are using manure hotbeds, this is not the case.

The crops that grow best in solar intensive gardens are leafy greens and root crops. Cold hardiness and short time to maturity are characteristics to look for when choosing varieties. If the seed package says "Wait until all danger of frost is past" before planting, the crop you have chosen is not a good one for the solar intensive garden.

Plants that require pollination to develop fruit (cucumbers, melons, tomatoes, etc.) are not good choices for the early spring intensive garden. They

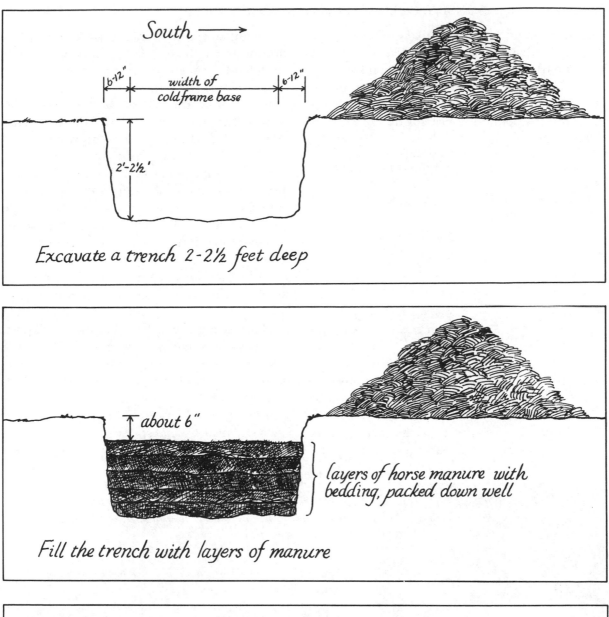

South ⟶

6-12"  width of cold frame base  6-12"

2'-2½'

Excavate a trench 2-2½ feet deep

about 6"

layers of horse manure with bedding, packed down well

Fill the trench with layers of manure

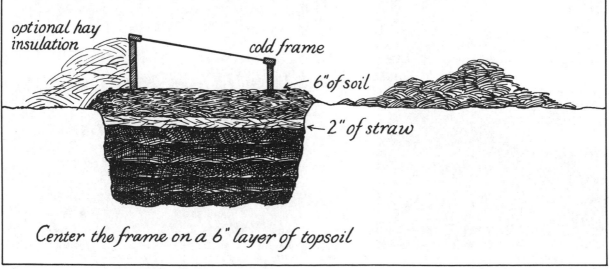

optional hay insulation

cold frame

6" of soil

2" of straw

Center the frame on a 6" layer of topsoil

**Figure 137**  *Building a manure bed.*

may be transplanted into intensive devices later in the spring, and can often be used to follow the harvest of earlier greens and root vegetables.

The following crops can be planted or transplanted into insulated or manure-heated beds up to three months before the last spring frost:

| lettuce: | spinach: |
|---|---|
| Oak leaf | Winter Bloomsdale |
| Grand Rapids Forcing | Bloomsdale |
| Arctic King | Monnopa |
| and other leafy types | and other varieties |
| carrots | India mustard |
| beets | Chinese cabbage |
| cauliflower | endive |
| broccoli | parsley |
| radishes | onion transplants |
| Swiss chard | strawberries |
| peas | |

We have tried many of these with varying success. Our greatest praise goes to the Chinese cabbages. They grow consistently through the coldest weather, and do quite well under glass. Swiss chard is also a winner as an early spring crop. The most difficult crops tend to be spinach, broccoli, and other cabbage family plants. One way to assure good lettuce is to start seedlings in the house or greenhouse and then move them into the garden after they are well established. We prefer leaf lettuce because it can be partially harvested continually and will continue to grow back.

All of these crops can be started as well later in the spring under cloches. About a month before the normal planting date you can plant seeds directly in the garden, many of them under the prewarmed soil of a cloche. Be sure to plant generously, then thin out the space until you have one plant per cloche. If you are using continuous cloches that form tunnels, the thinning process should result in the spacing recommended on the seed package.

Heat-loving crops like tomatoes, peppers, eggplant, melons, cucumbers, and squash can be set out about four weeks before the last frost date under either cloches, lights, or cold frames (devices that can be removed once the plants are well established) (see Figures 138 and 139). It is best to use only healthy transplants that are not leggy or sappy, because, although nighttime temperatures

PHOTO BY LEANDRE POISSON.

**Figure 138**  *Cantaloupes can get an early start when cloches are used to protect them from cool nighttime temperatures and to provide them with extra solar heat on cool days.*

**Figure 139**  *Cantaloupes in a cold frame in the garden of David Emery in Maine.*

PHOTO BY TIMOTHY FISHER.

under the cloches will not normally get down to freezing, weak plants can be seriously hampered by temperatures in the 30's and 40's.

## PLANT CARE

Once your plants are in the ground, you will need to tend them more carefully than you would in the summer garden. Thinning must be done regularly to prevent crowding. If you are interplanting, you will have to watch individual crops and pick them at the peak of maturity in order not to hamper neighboring crops by shading or competition for nutrients. You should also be prepared with a succession planting plan so that once an early crop is removed, it can be followed by another.

Temperature control is the real key to success. Cloches, lights, cold frames, Pods, or any solar intensive device must be ventilated to prevent excessively high temperatures on warm spring days. This ventilation is also necessary to reduce dampness, which could otherwise lead to mildew or fungal disease problems. Excessively high temperatures cause stress and wilting in some plants because photosynthesis increases with temperature. As it gets hotter, the plant may not be able to get enough water from the cooler ground to supply the photosynthesis process, and the leaves will wilt. This can cause further stress within the plant tissues and result in delayed maturity or, in extreme cases, death (see Figure 140).

Your objective should be to obtain daily temperatures that approximate the optimum growing conditions of the individual species. For most early spring crops this means no higher than 80° F and no lower than 40° F. Most gardeners worry more about cold temperatures than hot, but excess heat is actually more harmful to plants than cold.

Jim Crockett, the nationally known garden expert, suggested some guidelines for ventilating cold frames which are equally valid for other solar intensive devices. He suggested that when the outside temperatures reach 40° F, the cover should be opened about 6 inches. When the outdoor temperature gets up to 60° F, it is time to open the cover all the way. He noted that after midday (when there are a few hours of sun left) you should close the cover again to trap heat for the night.[1]

Any appropriate size piece of wood can be used to prop up covers of lights, cold frames, or Pods, but small notched props should be used to tilt up cloches during the day. They can be made with two or three settings so that the warmer it gets, the higher you can raise the cloche.

[1] Nancy Bubel. "Cold Frames and Hot Beds," *Horticulture*, vol. LVIII, no. 1, January 1980, p. 86.

**Figure 140** *Unless this Solar Pod is manually opened on sunny days, temperatures inside can get too high for good plant health.*

PHOTO BY LEANDRE POISSON.

The exception to these guidelines comes with your heat-loving crops. You can let them get a bit warmer than greens and root crops without doing any damage. Nonetheless, you should ventilate them somewhat to keep moisture from causing problems. The maximum temperature you should allow for these crops is about 90° F. Interestingly, we have grown squash under cone-shaped cloches in which the temperature got as high as 105° F. The cones have a small opening at the top that allows some air in, but we did not tip up the cone to allow air in at the bottom. The squash grew faster than neighboring, uncovered plants and did not suffer any apparent damage. As the plants grew too big for the cones, they were removed, and the flowering process began within a few days. The crop from the cone-covered plants was a full two weeks earlier than the neighboring, uncovered plants in the same bed.

On the other hand, beans and corn that were allowed to stay under cones at such high temperatures not only suffered from the experience, they died. Eggplant started under cones grew faster during the early part of the season, but did not produce a crop any sooner than the neighboring, uncovered plants.

Our best success has come with melons. We have grown them both in a solar hot frame and under cones. Both methods have produced startling results. In the hot frame we were able to produce extra early crops of melons that were almost free from pest problems. Apparently cucumber beetles, which are a great nuisance in our outdoor garden areas, do not like to fly under the covers of the hot frame and did not attack the plants. We kept the covers closed on cool nights; this meant that the air in the frame was usually 10 to 20 degrees warmer than the normal night air. During cooler days the covers were opened only about 6 inches. This kept the plants warmer than they would have been outdoors. In comparing the plants in the frame with those outdoors we found that the leaves of the frame plants were almost twice the size of the outdoor plants. Flowering was much earlier, and, with regular pruning, we were able to keep the plants flowering until early fall. The melons were larger, more numerous (on a per plant basis), and almost free of insect damage.

When cones were used, the melons were started indoors about four weeks before being set out into the garden. We used peat pots to eliminate any shock to the tender root system during transplanting. Setting out is done about two weeks before the last frost date. Each plant is then covered by a cone—all day on cool days (60° F or lower) and only during the morning on warmer days (60° F or higher). On warm days the cones were placed over the plants at midafternoon so that some warmth could be captured for overnight use. We left the cones on all day during cloudy periods.

After about two weeks under the cones, the plants had grown large enough almost to fill the cones. By the fourth week it became impossible to cover the plants with the cones any longer. The result of this effort has been flowering about two weeks before normal (for our climate) and a crop of melons two weeks before our usual mid-August harvest date.

Another important factor in plant care is watering. Usually it is not necessary early in the season because of the high moisture content of the soil and the general abundance of capillary water during spring thaw. As the season progresses, you should check the soil regularly. If it becomes dry more than 1 inch below the surface, you should water. Always water in the morning to make the moisture available to the plants for their daily photosynthesis. Evening watering results in excess moisture overnight and produces prime conditions for the development of mold and mildew.

If your plants show an obvious and urgent need for water during the day, be sure to use only warm water. "Warm water" is water that is at about the same temperature as the soil in your beds. Adding cold water will cool off the soil, making it harder for the plant to suck up the moisture from its roots into the leaves where it is needed.

## PESTS AND DISEASES

As we mentioned previously, the greatest disease threats to plants in solar intensive devices are the fungi and mildews caused by excessive moisture. Once you have these problems, they are difficult to eliminate. The first measure to take is to increase your ventilation and hope for dry weather. Secondly, you can try leaving the cover open a slight bit at night so that the relative humidity in the device will not increase to where moisture condenses on the surfaces and plants inside. If both these fail, your crop probably will too. The best thing to do then is pull it out and open up the device to allow it to be fully exposed to the sun for as long as it takes to dry it out completely. If your soil contains a soil-borne fungus or disease like verticillium, fusarium, or clubroot, you may want to dig out the soil and replace it.

Damping-off fungus is another potential problem in solar intensive devices, particularly in the early spring when your ventilation needs are low. Damping-off strikes young seedlings, causing them to become weak at the base of the stem and then fall over. The best control is prevention, and this is usually accomplished by spreading a thin layer of dry sand or sphagnum peat on the surface of the soil.

It is important to note that the tighter you build your devices the more moisture problem you are likely to have. "Not-so-tight" cold frames and uninsulated devices seem to have less of a problem with fungus and mildew. This may be because of air leakage, which prevents moisture levels from getting as high as they do in fully insulated and tightly sealed Pods and hot frames.

Crop rotation is essential in avoiding many diseases. One way to accomplish this is by having a number of solar intensive beds, so that you do not have to plant the same crop in one area more often than once every three years. This is particularly important in combating many of the diseases of the cabbage family. If you wish to build and maintain only one Pod, light, or cold frame cover, you can build a number of permanent beds to put it on. Then you can move the cover from bed to bed on a rotation. If building a number of beds is still too much work for you, then build one permanent bed and one cover, and rotate the soil by removing it at the end of each crop rotation. For example, if you are growing cabbage, then carrots, then peas, then lettuce, and back to cabbage again, you should change the soil before planting the cabbage for a second time (see Figure 141).

It is also a good idea to uncover a permanent bed once very few winters to let the soil freeze.

This will help bring some diseases under control and will destroy the larval stages of many insect pests.

Most common garden insect pests are not likely to be a problem in your solar intensive beds. This is because most insect pests have a specific life cycle that brings them out only when the season is right, usually in summer. Secondly, since your plants are growing in a protected environment, unless you inadvertently introduce a pest into your beds, it will usually not find its way in.

Even so, there are some particular pests to look out for (see Figure 142). Slugs will seek any warm moist place, and seem to have an affinity for solar intensive devices. We have had continual slug problems in our permanent beds. There are a number of home remedies for this problem, but we have tried only two. The first is to place a shallow pan of beer at ground level inside your device. The theory is that the slugs will smell or sense the beer and dive in for a drink. The little devils reportedly become intoxicated and forget how to swim, drowning in their stupor. As you may have guessed, this method has not worked for us, although some other gardeners swear by it. Maybe our slugs are teetotalers.

The method that works for us is a bit more demanding, but much more successful. Slugs like to hide under any object that traps the heat of the soil, and they also will climb to the top of a solar device to seek out the warmth that rises there at night. Our efforts at slug control concentrate upon placing boards on the soil, which attract the slugs. On a warm day (so the plants will not be damaged by opening the cover of the device) we go out and collect the slimy pests from under the boards. On warm nights they seem to congregate near the top of the device, on the walls and glass, and we pick them off there too. It is always good to check the plant leaves on warm evenings because some slugs are likely to be feeding there as well.

The other common pests of solar intensive gardens are aphids and whiteflies. These two insects are close relatives and like the same conditions. In most northern climates the winter is harsh enough that not many of these pests survive the cold. But in an intensive bed covered for the winter they can survive quite well. They thrive as the spring begins

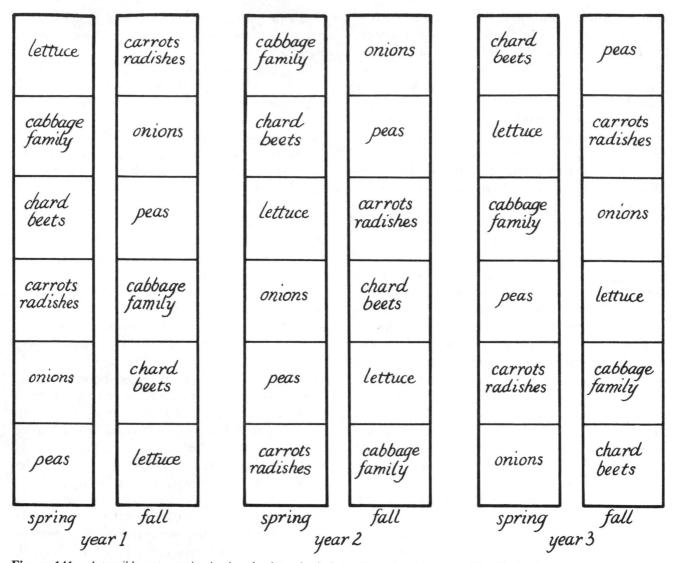

**Figure 141** *A possible crop rotation in six solar intensive beds (or in sections of large beds). The key is to avoid planting the same crop in one space more often than once every three years.*

to warm the environment of the solar intensive device, and your crops can become covered with them in what seems like no time at all. There are a few ways to control them, but you probably won't entirely eliminate them no matter what you do.

The first control to try is placing a piece of bright yellow-colored metal or paper under your plants. Coat the paper or metal with a sticky substance. For unknown reasons aphids and whiteflies are attracted to yellow and will become stuck to the trap you have made.

If the first method doesn't work, you can resort to more active control, using pyrethrum or rote-

none. Both of these will work to some degree (pyrethrum works the best), but neither will destroy all the pests. You will have to keep after them with occasional spraying or dusting until you can open up the bed in warmer weather. There are also some types of soaps that will kill aphids and whiteflies. Once the bed is exposed to the natural environment, the many predators (including ladybugs) upon these little insects can go to work and keep them under control for you. The use of predatory insects, for example certain species of tiny wasps (such as *Encarsia formosa*), works well in a green house environment, but in the environment

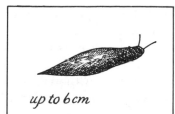

**SLUGS**
*slimey shelless snails which
have many tiny teeth and
are nocturnal feeders.*

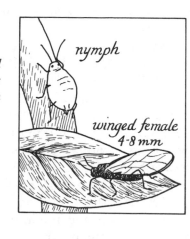

**Figure 142** *Slugs, aphids, and
whiteflies are the most common pests
of solar intensive devices in northern
climates.*

**APHIDS**
*The adults are dark colored
and nymphs are light green.*

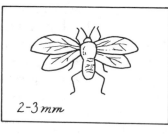

**WHITEFLIES** *minute white
insects covered by a white
powder. They are easily
disturbed and take wing at
the slightest movement.*

of solar intensive devices, these predators are unlikely to be able to maintain themselves. Wasps require warmer temperatures for reproduction than you are likely to have in your devices. In the long run, the best way to combat aphids and whiteflies is to enrich your soil with organic matter. A high humus content discourages both of these pests.

## THE SOLAR INTENSIVE GARDEN IN FALL

Fall gardening under glass works much the same way as in the spring except that it requires more attention to planting dates. While the early crops of spring benefit from the improving weather and longer days of April, May, and June, your fall

crops will find themselves working against rapidly shortening days, with colder day and night temperatures as the season progresses. This means you must plan your fall garden during the heat of summer and plant your crops early enough in the fall for them to be almost mature when winter arrives.

Certain crops are very sensitive to the photoperiod, or length of day. Onions, for example, will not bulb unless days are twelve hours or longer. Other plants flower only during days that are longer than the nights, and some plants will not produce foliage at all during the eight- to ten-hour daylight period of deep winter. This may be because of biological clocks in some plants set to put the plant into a dormant period during shorter, colder weather, or because the amount of light received during short days is inadequate to allow the plant to produce enough extra nourishment (plant sugars) to do much more than just survive. Whatever the reason, in northern climates most plants grow slowly or not at all during late December and January. You should bear this in mind when planning the fall planting schedule.

We recommend that you begin your fall planting of greens and root crops four to six weeks before the first expected frost. Continued planting at one- to two-week intervals until about a month after your first frost will generally result in a constant harvest right up until the coldest days of the winter.

In our southern New Hampshire garden we finish our fall planting around the beginning of October. This results in almost mature greens by the beginning of December, and these plants will be picked through January until they are almost gone. We are careful to leave some foliage on each plant, and in early February growth begins again, and harvesting can continue right on to spring planting time.

Soil preparation is relatively simple. Prepare your beds as though you were going to plant a regular summer crop, but instead of using the normal dose of fertilizer, cut it by about one-third. This is done because plants grow slower in the fall and nutrients become available through the normal soil decomposition process at a slower pace. Also, you will not lose nutrients from excessive leaching by rain. Excess fertilization can result in "sappy" plants, which are more susceptible to frost and cold damage than normal plants. Be sure to add a good amount of well-decomposed organic matter at this time, since this will be your last opportunity until spring.

If your soil needs an additional boost during the winter because nutrient levels are too low, it is best to use very diluted liquid fertilizers. It is generally suggested that you use a low concentration of liquid fish or manure tea on a regular basis—that is, once a week or every two weeks—rather than a stronger solution in a one-shot application. If you are worried about nutrient levels, learn to recognize the early signs of plant nutrient deficiency or get out your test kit before rushing to the bottle of liquid fertilizer. It will pay to add only those nu-

trients that are needed to avoid an overdose of the others. See Chapter 2 on soil for more specifics on sources of nutrients.[2]

You can use manure hotbeds in the fall as well. Although the timing of the heat release is not well coordinated with the demands of your crops (the manure will be getting colder just as the coldest temperatures of fall arrive), this heat source can still be an advantage in uninsulated beds.

## SOLAR DEVICES FOR THE FALL

You can use the same solar devices in the fall that you used in the spring: Pods, cold frames, lights, and hot frames, with one possible exception, individual cloches. The problem with individual cloches is that they are generally too small to hold a maturing plant, and the point at which you need the protection of the cloche is as the plant is maturing in mid to late fall. Pods, cold frames, lights, and hot frames work better because they afford the space full-grown plants require and because they hold more heat through the night.

If you are in a relatively mild climate (such as is found in coastal areas or in states at about thirty-seven degrees north latitude or lower), you should be able to extend your growing season right through the fall without insulating your devices. In colder climates, as in New England, an insulated device is essential (see Figures 143–145). Insulation below ground helps keep soil temperatures warm enough to encourage continued growth even when outdoor temperatures begin to hover in the 30's. See Chapter 6, "Solar Intensive Devices," for insulation details.

A device we are particularly happy with for fall and winter gardening is the solar hot frame. It is essentially a solar-heated "hot house" and is capable of carrying many crops right through the winter in all but subarctic climates. It is used in the same way as Pods or cold frames, but is much more completely insulated. A unique feature of this type of device is an insulated shutter which

[2] A useful guide to recognizing deficiencies is "A Key to Nutrient Disorders of Vegetable Plants" by Jean English and Donald N. Maynard in *Hortscience,* Vol. 13 (1), Feb. 1978.

**Figure 143** *Solar Pods can be used to extend the season well into the winter months. Garden of Leandre and Gretchen Poisson in New Hampshire.*

**Figure 144** *Solar Pods in the Poisson's winter garden in New Hampshire.*

**Figure 145** *Solar Pods in the Poisson's winter garden in New Hampshire.*

covers the plants at night, preventing excessive heat loss through the glazing. We have successfully grown many leafy crops, root crops, herbs, and cabbage family plants through winters in New Hampshire, where temperatures of 20°F to 30°F below zero are frequent.

A device with a single glazing will allow you to produce harvests until nighttime temperatures drop below around 20°F. Double-glazed devices can protect most leafy crops down to about 10°F. Once the temperature drops below this, most crops will be frosted enough to die back unless you cover your device with some kind of insulation for the night. Although we have not tried it, we suspect that double-glazed Pods and cold frames could protect mature crops down to about 0°F outdoor temperature if the glazing were covered with heavy blankets, loose hay, or straw.

Be sure to check your devices for leaks and drafts. A small leak can lose enough heat to make the difference between survival or freezing for many crops. If you find any leaks, you can use small pieces of foam rubber, string, or cloth to seal them up.

If you use a device through the winter, you may find that the frost in the ground can twist it or push it out of shape. This can lead to loose fits on your covers and result in air leaks. To prevent this you can either treat the symptoms by plugging leaks as they appear or build the base of your device with deep insulation or a masonry foundation.

## CROP SELECTION

We have found that many of the same crops that grow well in the spring intensive garden also do well in the fall.

Below are some crops that are particularly good performers in the fall garden:

†*Chinese cabbage (see below)
leaf lettuce
   †Arctic King
   Black Seeded Simpson
   cos or romaine
   *Grand Rapids Forcing
   *Oak Leaf
†*Swiss chard
†*kale

†endive
†*parsley
*radishes
†turnips
†*spinach

Other crops that can be used are:

*broccoli
*beets
*corn salad (mache)
collards
kress
*escarole
celery
cabbage
mustard greens
*carrots
rutabagas
cauliflower
bunching and scallion onions
leeks
*and many perennial herbs

There are also some unusual oriental plants that grow well in fall intensive gardens. They are well suited to the short days and seem to be able to grow even when other crops are dormant. They are:

*†Siew Choy cabbage (heading)
*Bok Choy cabbage (leafy)
Wong Bok cabbage (heading)
Daikon radish
Gai Lohn (Chinese broccoli or kale)
Gow Choy (Chinese chives)
†Shungiku (Edible Chrysanthemum)
†Dai Gai Choy (Gai Choy) (Indian mustard)
†Pak Choy (white cabbage)
†Kyo Mizuna
†Seppaku Tiana (leaf cabbage)
†Komatsuna (leaf cabbage)
†Choy Sum (flowering white cabbage)
Heung Kum (Chinese celery)
Yuen Sai (Chinese parsley)

* Indicates plants we have successfully grown through the winter in a solar hot frame.

† Indicates plants that have been successfully grown through the winter at the Rodale Organic Gardening Research Center in Emmaus, Pennsylvania. These plants were grown in the Rodale Solar Growing Frame.[3]

[3] Ray Wolf, ed. *Rodale's Solar Growing Frame* (Emmaus, Pa.: Rodale Press, 1980).

A list of companies that sell some or all of the oriental vegetables is included at the end of this chapter.

## PLANT CARE

It is difficult to give specific instructions on planting dates for fall solar intensive crops. Shorter days make the plants grow slower and extend the estimated "date to maturity" figures listed on seed packages. Additionally, cooler soil and air temperatures make it harder for plants to use the light they do get efficiently. We have estimated that in determining when to plant most leafy crops you should add at least 20 to 40 percent to the "date to maturity" figures listed on the package. For root crops planted early in the fall you should add the same, but if your root crops go in late (after mid-September where we are), you may have to wait until late winter and early spring for a harvest.

We have found that lettuce and chard started in late September will take as much as three months to reach maturity in the New Hampshire climate. By December there is so little light that most leafy crops simply stop growing altogether. If you are using Pods, lights, or cold frames, this is the time to harvest, since no further growth is likely. In the hot frame you can leave the plants in the ground, and they will provide occasional harvests until they begin to grow again in early February. By early March production should be going strong. In mild climates some growth will occur during the entire winter, and with some trial and error you will probably be able to develop a planting schedule that will yield fresh produce the full twelve months of the year.

You should keep all fall and winter crops well thinned. Crowding is particularly harmful, as it will cause plants to become leggy and weak-stemmed. Spacing should be slightly farther apart than in the summer garden to allow each plant to obtain full sun. A good rule of thumb would be to add 2 to 4 inches to the normal intensive planting spacings shown in Chapter 3.

Weeds are rarely a problem in glazed beds. Occasionally some leftover weed seeds from the summer will germinate in the warm environment of the solar intensive device. These few stragglers will rarely grow to maturity and almost never go to seed. You should pull them, however, because they will shade the soil and reduce the heating that is so important to maintaining warm soil temperatures.

Watering will be necessary early in the fall when plants are still strong. Since daytime temperatures are still high (above 60° F), you will not be covering the beds except at night. This will result in enough water loss to require regular sprinkling. However, as temperatures drop and you are keeping the covers on your beds during the day, the need for water will diminish. Do not water established crops unless you find that the soil is not damp within half an inch of the surface.

Further on into the winter watering needs will drop to almost nothing. This requires a cutback in your sprinkling efforts to prevent the creation of conditions conducive to disease and fungus development. Regular watering at this point can be more harmful than helpful. In New Hampshire the late fall months usually bring plenty of rain, which soaks the soil, and our problem becomes too much, not too little, water. This is partly due to capillary water, which moves upward into the soil of frames and Pods from the underground water table. In warm weather this capillary water evaporates at the soil surface, but in cold weather and in an enclosed solar intensive device the water cannot evaporate and escape as readily. This means that from late October to March we do not water at all. (We have a heavy clay subsoil; in sandy soils this may not be the case.)

Temperature control in fall is slightly different from what it is in spring. In spring soil and air temperatures just outside your solar intensive devices will be constantly increasing, so it is less crucial to conserve heat from the sun. In fall, with dropping air and soil temperatures, it is helpful to keep your devices closed more of the time to conserve valuable heat for nighttime use. This, on the other hand, can cause problems of overheating. Fortunately, overheating and the need to store heat for night can be addressed through the wise use of thermal mass.

Thermal mass is simply any massive material that can absorb and hold heat. Commonly used materials are water in drums or bottles and masonry such as concrete or bricks. Water holds almost four times as much heat per cubic foot as masonry, so it is desirable from a space-saving point of view. In either case, the function of thermal mass is to absorb some portion of the sun's energy that enters the solar intensive device, thus reducing the amount that immediately turns into hot air and increasing the amount held for release during the night as air temperatures drop.

Drums painted black and filled with water are commonly used in the Pod system. This allows the covers to be left closed most of the day during fall and spring. Our own solar hot frame contains three 30-gallon drums of water, which help store heat for overnight use. Other systems use concrete slabs imbedded under the hot frame, and some

schemes use rocks as the thermal storage medium (see Figure 146).

Even in cold periods, when heat is precious, some ventilation is necessary. Fresh air is beneficial because it allows the oxygen given off by plants to escape and carbon dioxide, which plants absorb during photosynthesis, to get in. Air movement also helps to prevent mold and mildew, as many greenhouse operators have discovered. You should allow some ventilation except on the coldest days. Opening the cover of your frame or Pod only a quarter of an inch can accomplish this, but be sure to do this only during the sunny period of the day. Be sure to close the cover again before the

**Figure 146** *Options for adding thermal mass to solar intensive devices.*

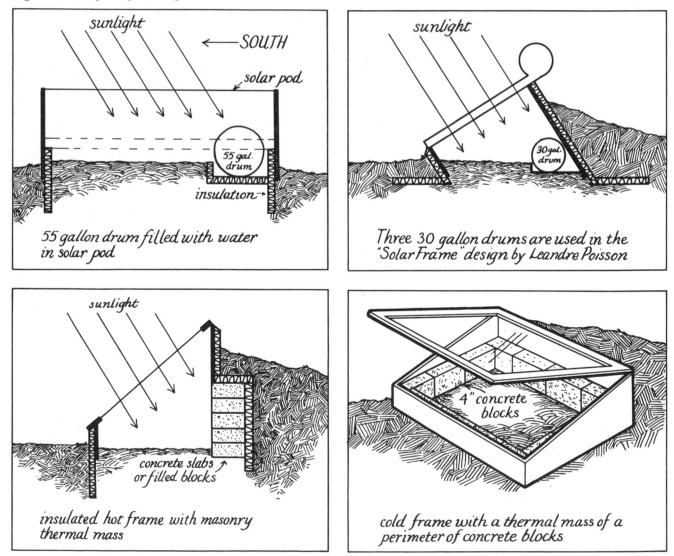

55 gallon drum filled with water in solar pod

Three 30 gallon drums are used in the "Solar Frame" design by Leandre Poisson

insulated hot frame with masonry thermal mass

cold frame with a thermal mass of a perimeter of concrete blocks

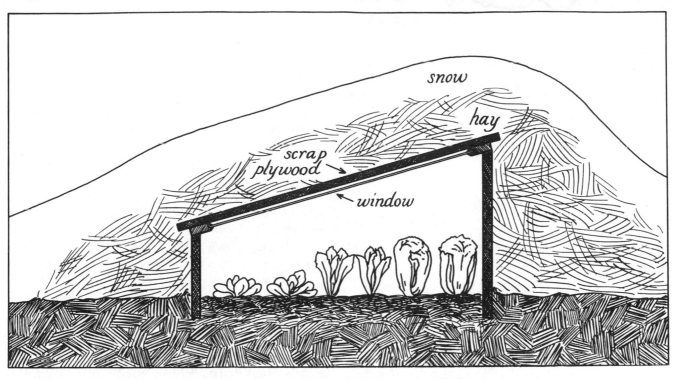

**Figure 147** *A cold frame covered with hay and snow will keep hardy greens through the winter.*

sun goes down so that enough heat will be held for the night. You should also try to ventilate in a way that doesn't let in cold blasts of air that hit the plants directly. A small ventilating hole, with a cover or plug, near the top of your device can help with this and may eliminate the need to crack open the cover itself.

It is important not to allow temperature to change too rapidly in your devices. If, for example, you find that the temperature in a cold frame has risen above the desired level, do not immediately throw open the cover. Allow a gradual temperature drop by propping the cover open a little for about half an hour and then a little more for another half an hour until the temperature reaches the desired level. A sudden drop in temperature is damaging to plants, and a rapid change in relative humidity caused by allowing all the moisture in the device to escape quickly is equally bad. Such sudden changes usually cause wilting and can reduce plant vigor and set back growth.

## CROPS FOR WINTERING-OVER IN UNINSULATED DEVICES

If you do not build a fully insulated structure like the solar hot frame, or if you want to use your cold frames, Pods, and lights through the winter, you can employ them as wintering-over equipment. Certain crops that will not survive the winter in open gardens will do admirably with the protection provided by these devices. They will not grow much or at all during the winter, but in early spring will be awakened to begin a new year's growth.

The procedure is the same as for producing a fall crop, only you do not harvest the plants and you can usually start planting a little later. You should not harvest or take cuttings from your overwintering crops after they have been exposed to a frost because cutting encourages further growth. What you want to do is get the plant to the point where it is almost mature and then let it go into a dormant stage for the winter. Once the daily temperatures stay below freezing, you should cover the glazing with a material that will cut out solar energy. This will prevent any warm sunny periods in midwinter from reawakening the plants prematurely (see Figure 147).

If you live in an area where there is a lot of snow, be sure to provide some support for the glazing to prevent the weight of the snow from breaking the glass or fiberglass. In early spring, once the days get into the 40's and the daylight is about eleven or twelve hours long, you can uncover the device and allow the sun to shine in. In no time the crops will spring to life and within a

105

few weeks you will be able to harvest. Some crops to try overwintering for spring harvest are:

cabbage
Chinese cabbage
Swiss chard
beet greens
kress
parsley
broccoli
cauliflower
bunching onions and scallions
parsnips
carrots
kale
garlic
and perennial herbs

You can also overwinter crops in your summer garden by covering them with cloches or a heavy mulch. Most root crops can be saved until spring this way, parsnips being one of the most notable. We have also mulched onions, carrots, herbs, parsley, and Swiss chard with success.

## SOME WORDS OF CAUTION

We recommend starting small. Solar intensive gardening demands more of the gardener than summer gardening. Your timing and scheduling of planting, thinning, and harvesting requires more thought than in summer. Frequent trips into the garden are absolutely essential because one day of overheating can severely injure or even kill many crops. If you have devices with insulating covers, you will have to remember to open them every morning and close them every night. You must consciously refrain from watering and fertilizing as often as you do in summer. The more advanced solar intensive devices are somewhat expensive and time-consuming to build, so don't overextend yourself until you have had success on a small scale. Finally, you must keep your equipment in good condition, and that requires regular maintenance throughout the year.

One of the biggest demands of solar intensive gardens is the constant diligence required to maintain optimum temperatures in the devices.

Many days we have had to make frequent trips into the garden to accommodate the fickle ways of the weather. If the day is one when the sun appears briefly and then disappears, only to return again a few hours later, you will have to make a number of journeys to your devices. All this running back and forth can get to be pretty tedious. It can be particularly bothersome when you want to go away for a weekend, or if you are a working person who is away all day. Either you will have to train your neighbors to babysit your garden or invest in only those devices that can be operated by automatic openers.

Starting out small will minimize the initial problems you will run into. It is much better to go through the trial-and-error stage in one or two Pods, cold frames, or hot frames than in dozens of them. Once you have a season of experience, you can then expand in whatever ways have proven to be the most successful for you.

## SOURCES FOR COLD-HARDY VEGETABLE VARIETIES

The following companies sell varieties of cold-hardy vegetables that can be used in solar intensive devices. This list was compiled by Steve Tracy at the Ashland Community Organic Gardening Project in Ashland, Massachusetts.

BURGESS SEEDS
P. O. Box 218
Galesburg, MI 49053
BURPEE SEEDS
Warminster, PA 18001
DESSERT SEED CO.
P. O. Box 181
El Centro, CA 92243
DOMINION SEEDS
Georgetown, Ontario L7G 4A2
EPICURE SEEDS
Box 69
Avon, NY 10538
GRACE'S GARDENS
Autumn Lane
Hackettstown, NJ 07840
GURNEY'S SEED AND NURSERY CO.
Yankton, SD 57078

HERBST BROTHERS SEEDSMEN, INC.
100 N. Main St.
Brewster, NY 10509

J. A. DEMONCHAUX CO.
225 Jackson
Topeka, KA 66603

J. L. HUDSON, SEEDSMAN
P. O. Box 1058
Redwood City, CA 94064

JAPONICA NURSERY
Seed Department
P. O. Box 69
Larchmont, NY 10538

LE JARDIN DU GOURMET
West Danville, VT 05873

JOHNNY'S SELECTED SEEDS
Albion, ME 04910

LOWDEN'S BETTER SEEDS AND PLANTS
Box 10
Ancaster, Ontario L9G 3L3

MCFAYDEN SEED CO., LTD.
P. O. Box 1600
30 Ninth St.
Brandon, Manitoba R7A 6A6

THE ORIENTAL COUNTRY STORE
12 Mott St.
New York, NY 10013

PELLETT GARDENS
Atlantic, IA 50022

R. H. SHUMWAY
Rockford, IL 61101

ROSWELL SEED CO.
115–117 S. Main
Roswell, NM 88201

STOKES SEED CO.
737 Main St.
Box 548
Buffalo, NY 04240

TSANG AND MA INTERNATIONAL
P. O. Box 294
Belmont, CA 94002

WILLIAM DAM SEEDS
West Flamboro, Ontario
LOR 2KO

## REFERENCES AND FURTHER READINGS:

AQUATIAS, A. *Intensive Culture of Vegetables on the French System* (Harrisville, N.H.: Solar Survival, 1978, reprint of 1913 ed.). *An early description of the French market gardening system as practiced around Paris in the early 1900's. Includes detailed descriptions of devices and horticultural practices.*

CARTER, A. R. *Dutch Lights for Growers and Gardeners* (London: Vinton, 1956).

CHASE, J. L. H. *Commercial Cloche Gardening* (London: Faber and Faber, 1952). *A very useful book with information on many facets of both cold and warm season gardening, by the originator of the continuous cloche.*

COLEBROOK, BINDA. *Winter Gardening in the Maritime Northwest* (Tilth Association, 1977). *Includes a good list of winter crops and how to grow them.*

COPLEY, GEORGE H. *Growing under Glass* (London: John Crowther, 1945). *Probably out of print.*

DAKERS, J. S. *Early Vegetables under Glass* (London: Cassell, 1936). *Out of print.*

FLAWN, LOUIS. *Gardening with Cloches* (London: John Gifford, 1957, 1967). *A very good book on a wide variety of cloches and how to use them.*

*Getting the Most from Your Garden.* The editors of *Organic Gardening* magazine (Emmaus, Pa.: Rodale, 1980). *A very useful and complete reference on all aspects of intensive gardening, including a chapter on "Extending Your Growing Season."*

MCCULLAGH, JAMES (ed.). *The Solar Greenhouse Book* (Emmaus, Pa.: Rodale, 1978). *Contains a section on season-extending devices by Leandre Poisson, and information on materials used in constructing solar intensive devices.*

QUARRELL, C. P. *Intensive Salad Production* (London: Crosby Lockwood, 1938). *Another English book that describes and documents the development of gardening under glass in the early twentieth century.*

SPICE, HENRY. *Polyethylene Film in Horticulture* (London: Faber and Faber, 1959). *Probably out of print, but worth searching for, because it has many good (and some unusual) ideas for building inexpensive solar intensive devices.*

WEATHERS, JOHN. *French Market Gardening* (London: John Murray, 1909). *Out of print. This is probably the first English book on gardening under glass; it is one of the best. It fully documents the methods of the French* maraîchers.

WILLMOTT, P. K. *Dutch Lights and Frames* (London: Ernest Benn, 1958).

## OTHER SOURCES OF INFORMATION:

COMMUNITY ORGANIC GARDENING PROJECT, Ashland Educational Community Center, Ashland, Mass. 01721. *C.O.G. has conducted tests on a variety of solar intensive devices and has published results of their work.*

THE COOLIDGE CENTER FOR THE ADVANCEMENT OF AGRICULTURE, Riverhill Farm, Topsfield, Mass. 01983. *The C.C.A.A. is conducting research on Dutch Light systems for market gardeners and farmers.*

NEW ALCHEMY INSTITUTE, 237 Hatchville Road, East Falmouth, Mass. 02536. *New Alchemy writes an annual Journal published by The Stephen Greene Press, which frequently includes information on solar intensive methods.*

RODALE ORGANIC GARDENING AND FARMING RESEARCH CENTER, RD#1, Box 323, Kutztown, Penn. 19530. *The Rodale Center has conducted numerous tests on cold frames, hot frames, and other solar intensive devices. They have excellent knowledge of crop selection and horticultural techniques.*

SOLAR SURVIVAL, Box 119, Harrisville, N.H. 03450. *Founded by Leandre Poisson, Solar Survival has developed numerous devices for season-extending and sells plans for some of their inventions.*

# 6

# SOLAR INTENSIVE DEVICES

Paul Doscher

A SOLAR intensive device, as we have defined it, is any garden enclosure that captures solar heat and in turn allows the creation of a modified climate in which plants can be grown. We clearly draw a distinction between the artificial climate of greenhouses and solar greenhouses, which are much more controlled environments, and the less controllable, modified climate inside a solar intensive device.

There are countless ways to produce the microclimate needed for solar intensive gardening. This chapter is not intended to discuss each and every one, but rather to offer a general catalog of the types and uses of the more common and most effective devices we have seen or used. It will also provide some general guidelines for the construction and maintenance of solar devices and accessories.

## CLOCHES

The cloche, as originated in Europe, is a small, plant-sized glass or plastic device designed to create a more temperate microclimate during the period just before and after the normal, frost-free growing season. It is a very simple device, and in most cases the least expensive to own and use.

The bell cloche was the mainstay of the early French intensive gardeners (see Figure 148). These cloches were made of glass tinted slightly blue; stood about 17 inches high and 15 inches in diameter. Because they were heavy (5½ pounds each) and fragile, the French had special racks for carrying them. Unfortunately, these glass jar enclosures could easily be broken. A damaged cloche was usually repaired using lead, something not recommended today when we know of the health hazards associated with this toxic metal. New cloches were purchased by the case, and many early intensive gardeners bought them in quantities of a hundred or more every year.

The bell cloche was used for a number of purposes:

Protecting seedlings from the wind;
Prewarming soil before planting or transplanting;
Protection of both young and mature plants from light frosts;
Protection of plants during excessively damp or

109

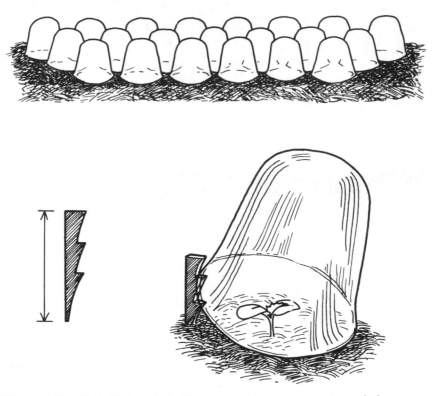

**Figure 148** *Bell Cloches: (A) Three rows of cloches arranged on a bed; (B) Wooden tilt for cloches; (C) A cloche and tilt.*

rainy weather;

Protection of plants from animal pests;

Provision of an optimum growing temperature during cooler weather.

Often a grower could start a number of seedlings under one cloche and then transplant them as they grew larger into individual cloches. In the mild French climate lettuce, cabbages, cauliflower, and other foliage crops could be brought to maturity entirely under cloches.

There are disadvantages to this type of cloche, however:

Overheating is possible if the cloche is not "tipped" during warm days. A small "tilt" was used by the French for this purpose (see Figure 148).

The cloche could not protect a plant from a heavy frost.

The glass cloches were heavy and fragile, resulting in frequent breakages and difficulty in providing suitable storage space.

It is unlikely that you will find any of the original French-type cloches today. However, it is possible to make modern versions of the cloche using old pickle jars and other glass containers large enough to hold a full-grown plant.

### The Jug Cloche

This is an inexpensive and reasonably effective substitute for the glass version. For better or worse, juices, milk, cider, and other fluids all seem to come in plastic jugs these days. Rather than throw them away, a solar intensive gardener can cut off the bottoms and use them for protecting small seedlings and transplants (see Figure 149). Most jugs are only about 6 inches square at the base and are made of translucent plastic, which makes them useful for growing small plants, though too tiny for mature ones.

When using jug cloches, you should leave off the caps to allow a small amount of ventilation. Some gardeners replace the caps at night, but this is

**Figure 149**  *Milk jug cloches.*

certainly an odd sight, but for the price the jug can't be beat as a mini solar intensive device.

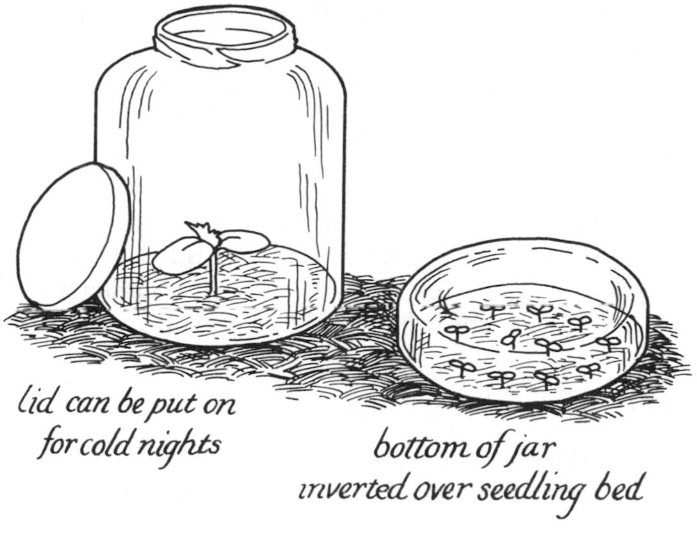

Glass jars can also be made into jug-type cloches. it is harder to cut the bottoms off, but they certainly will not blow away in the wind.

You can buy a commercially available bottle-cutting jig to remove the jar bottom. Alternatively, you can tie a kerosene-soaked cotton string tightly around the jar about 2 inches above the base. Then light the string with a match, and when the fire has burned itself out, pour a little cold water on the bottle. It should break along the line where the string was. Use a little sandpaper to smooth the edge before using this glass cloche in your garden.

The bottom of the bottle, which looks like a shallow glass bowl, can also be used. Inverted over a newly seeded area, it will give the seeds a warm microclimate to sprout in (see Figure 150).

probably unnecessary unless a frost is expected. Because they are so light and easily blown over, it is impractical to tilt open a jug cloche on warm days, and so they must be removed to prevent overheating.

If a strong wind comes up, the jugs will blow away unless they are firmly pressed into the ground. If this doesn't hold them, you will have to attach the handles to wooden stakes.

A garden covered with dozens of milk jugs is

*Hot Caps*

These are inexpensive, waxed-paper cloches, and are available in many garden stores and from seed catalogs. They work the same as any other cloche, but have the disadvantage of being very fragile and short-lived. Their unique advantage is that they are ventilated by opening the folds of the waxed paper at the top. This allows them to be "permanently" set into the soil (see Figure 151). Prices vary, but a box of a hundred usually sells for between $10 and $15.

**Figure 150**  *Glass jar cloche.*

*lid can be put on for cold nights*

*bottom of jar inverted over seedling bed*

**Figure 151**  *Hotcaps are available in most garden stores and catalogs; they are useful but short-lived.*

**Figure 152** *Solar cones of various sizes can be made from sheets of fiberglass-reinforced plastic.*

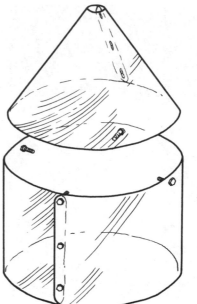

*1" long ⅛" bolt and nut about 1" below rim*

**Figure 154** *A solar cone riser. This cylinder, made of the same material as the cone, can allow more space for growing plants. It is made with a piece of fiberglass-reinforced plastic formed into a cylinder just slightly larger than the base of the cone. Small bolts are inserted through the riser so that the cone rests on them when it is set into the cylinder.*

## The Solar Cone

Designed by Leandre Poisson of Harrisville, New Hampshire, the cone is quite unique and very simple (see Figure 152). It is made from a semi-rigid, fiberglass-reinforced plastic developed for use on solar collectors. The material is cut in the shape of a semicircle, and the straight edges are then drawn together and fastened to form the cone (see Figure 153). Wing nuts or brass paper fasteners can be used to do this.

An advantage of this device is that it can be made in almost any size you need. Additionally, the material they are made from is virtually indestructible and will last for ten to fifteen years with minimal care. The small hole at the top of the cone allows some ventilation on mild days, eliminating the need to tip it up to prevent overheating.

On the other hand, the little hole is inadequate for ventilation on warmer days, so the cones must be removed to prevent overheating. Another disadvantage is that the sloping sides of the cone do not allow room for many plants to grow to maturity (see Figures 154 and 155). Lastly, it should be mentioned that the material the cones are made from commonly costs between 65¢ and 75¢ per square foot, making a small, 16-inch diameter cone cost between $1.80 and $2.25 to build.

**Figure 153** *Pattern for cutting solar cones.*

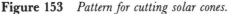
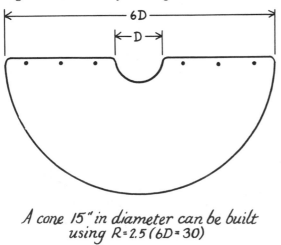

*A cone 15" in diameter can be built using R=2.5 (6D = 30)*

## The Continuous Cloche

According to the early intensive gardeners of England, the bell cloche was unworkable because

112

PHOTO BY PAUL DOSCHER.

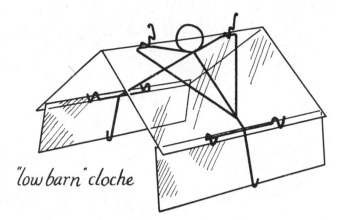

"low barn" cloche

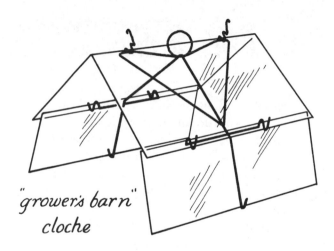

"grower's barn" cloche

Figure 155  *A solar cone with riser.*

of its fragility and size. In response to this criticism, Mr. L. H. Chase invented the continuous cloche, which is constructed of panes of glass and which allowed a long row of plants to be enclosed under a single device.

The continuous cloche, still available today, comes in two types: the tent and the barn. Both are constructed using sheets of glass 12 inches by 24 inches and wire supports to hold the glass in place.

Tent cloches have the advantage of being simple and relatively inexpensive, but have the problem of sloping sides that cramp growing plants. Barn cloches with low, medium, or high side walls provide more growing space and the feature of opening sides for daytime ventilation (see Figure 156). For further height, continuous cloches can be raised up on bricks or wood blocks.

An advantage of the continuous cloche is that provided by shifting an entire row of cloches from one crop, as it matures, to another younger crop just beside it. This works well for gardens where

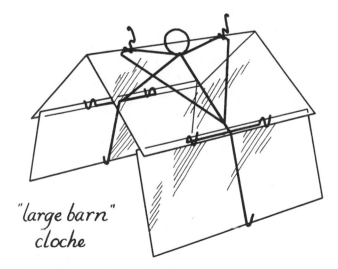

"large barn" cloche

Figure 156  *Three barn cloche designs.*

**Figure 157** *Glass cloches in use for warming tomatoes at the Coolidge Center for the Advancement of Agriculture in Massachusetts. Unfortunately, if cloches are not adequately ventilated on hot days, plants can be damaged.*

PHOTO BY TIMOTHY FISHER.

crops are planted in rows (see Figure 157). In this way successive plantings of a crop benefit from the controlled environment of the enclosure, and the fragile glass material need not be moved a great distance or put into storage (see Figure 158).

Glass cloches of the Chase type can also be upended in early summer to serve as windbreaks for young tomato, pepper, eggplant, melon, or cucumber plants (see Figure 159). This promotes rapid growth while avoiding the potential for excessive temperatures.

Unfortunately, glass sells at premium prices today. A number of manufacturers and garden equipment suppliers sell hardware for tent and Chase-type cloches, but the largest expenditure for the cloche is the glass panes. When considering the potential for accidental breakage, it is likely that many gardeners are better served by choosing another type of cloche. This problem has been addressed by some new cloche designs constructed of durable transparent plastics, some of which are even double-walled. The new continuous designs are quite expensive also, costing about $20 to $25 for each section.

### The Tunnel Cloche

Many gardeners have developed their own versions of this popular enclosure. It is nothing more than a tunnel-shaped polyethylene plastic cover, supported by metal, rigid plastic, or wooden

114

arches. Polyethylene is inexpensive and has the advantage of being easy to move, store, and replace. The light allowed through polyethylene does not differ noticeably from that which passes through glass.

Almost any rigid framework can be used to construct tunnel cloches. A wood frame can be erected using scrap lumber or pieces of woody brush trimmed from trees or the scrubby growth at the edge of fields (see Figure 160). Metal coat hangers, bent to form an arch, are another common structure (see Figure 161). The frame should be firmly imbedded into the soil and the plastic attached or weighted down along the sides to prevent a gust of wind from blowing it off. Ends of the tunnel can be sealed when necessary with pieces of glass, boards, or sections of rigid plastic or fiberglass.

A problem with plastic tunnel cloches is ventilation. To provide adequate cooling the polyethylene must often be removed. The benefits of heat assistance and wind protection are then lost. Another drawback is the tendency of polyethylene to deteriorate when exposed to sunlight. This degradation results in the need to replace the material at least every few years, and possibly as often as every year. Nevertheless, the tunnel cloche is a very useful device because of its simplicity and low cost.

A new product in which chicken wire is molded in between two layers of polyethylene provides the

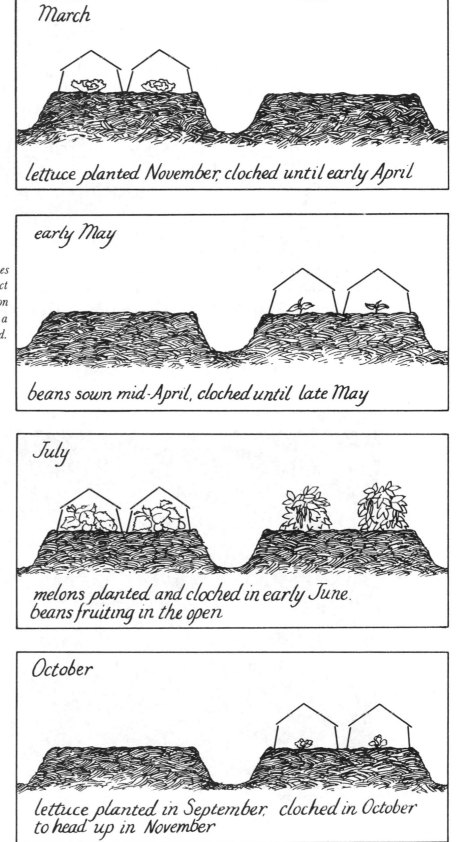

**Figure 158** *Continuous cloches can be used to protect crops throughout the season if they are moved in a rotation from bed to bed.*

**Figure 159** *Continuous glass cloches up-ended to provide wind protection for young plants.*

**Figure 160** *Arches made with brush wood can become a framework for tunnel cloches.*

PHOTO BY TIMOTHY FISHER.

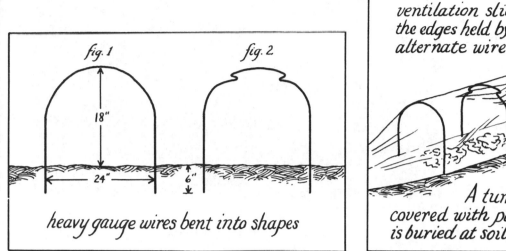

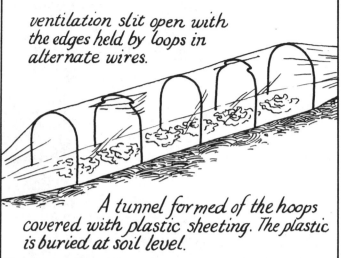

**Figure 161** *Heavy gauge wires can be used to form supports for polyethylene cloches.*

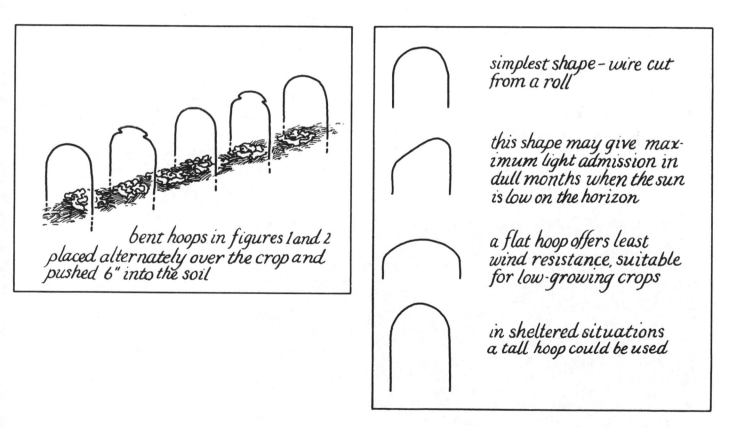

**Figure 162** *A simple tunnel cloche formed with a piece of fiberglass-reinforced plactic. The shape is held together with pieces of heavy gauge galvanized wire.*

PHOTO BY PAUL DOSCHER.

option of having cover and structure all in one. The material costs about $13 for a roll 3 feet wide by 25 feet long (1980 prices).

The same fiberglass material used to make cones can be used to form a tunnel cloche as well. This is done by cutting a long piece of the fiberglass and bending it into a U-shape, which is held together with coat hangers. This tunnel cloche is very long-lasting, but quite expensive compared to the polyethylene model (see Figure 162).

### The Tomato Cage Cloche

Many gardeners save space and labor by growing tomatoes in wire cages. These structures are generally 18 inches in diameter by 4 feet tall. They can be turned into a solar intensive shelter (which looks like a high-rise cloche) by wrapping the cage with a layer of polyethylene plastic. The plastic should be fastened tightly to the cage and the cage anchored firmly in the ground (see Figures 164 and 165). This device will allow you to set out tomatoes in their final growing places as much as three to four weeks before your normal planting date. It will protect plants from cool winds, excessive rains, and create the hot, humid climate that tomatoes love. During the day the top is uncovered, but on cool nights a board or piece of rigid fiberglass or glass is used to trap the heat inside.

Our neighbors in southern New Hampshire have used the tomato cage cloche for a number of years. They consistently report that their tomaotes flower and set fruit a full three weeks earlier than unprotected plants. Once the weather warms up for the summer, the plastic is removed to allow access to the ripening fruit.

PHOTO BY TIMOTHY FISHER.

**Figure 163** *Recycled materials can provide the structure for inexpensive cloche-type enclosures. This device built from the frame of a pick-up camper can also be covered with wooden slats to provide summer shading. Garden of Norman and Sherrie Lee in New York.*

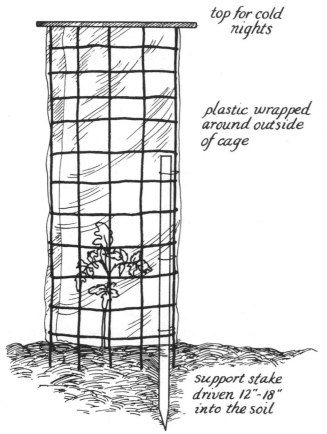

top for cold
nights

plastic wrapped
around outside
of cage

support stake
driven 12"-18"
into the soil

**Figure 164** *A tomato cage cloche can be used to extend the harvest or for giving the plants an extra early start in the spring.*

**Figure 165** *Tomato cage cloches in Janney Munsell's garden in Maine.*

## LIGHTS AND FRAMES

Dutch, French, and English lights and cold frames are all variations of a basic design including a wooden frame covered by a glass window. A number of them can be placed over an intensive bed to allow a large area to be enclosed. As an alternative, the bed can be framed by a permanent wooden structure, which both holds the soil and provides the base for the windows.

The minigreenhouse created by the lights allows crops to grow in a modified climate similar to that in cloches, but requiring less labor for maintaining proper moisture and ventilation.

### Dutch, French, English, and Early American Lights

Lights are devices originally developed for use in market gardening. We have described the sizes and construction of these devices in Chapter 1 (see also Figure 27).

During the early days of intensive market gardening the construction and sizes of lights became standardized in each country because of the substantial demand for this type of enclosure. At one time hundreds of acres of market gardens in Europe were covered by lights.

The basic parts of these devices were:

1. A bottomless frame (usually 3 to 4 feet wide by 4 to 6 feet long) built to be about 9 inches high on one side and about 6 inches high on the other, to allow for runoff of rain.
2. Windows, or "lights," to cover the entire wooden frame. They consisted of a wooden sash, and could each be glazed with one pane of glass (Dutch type) or many small panes (French, English, and American types) (see Figures 27, 166, and 167).
3. Straw or other types of mats used to cover the glass lights at night. These mats were used only if there was danger of frost.

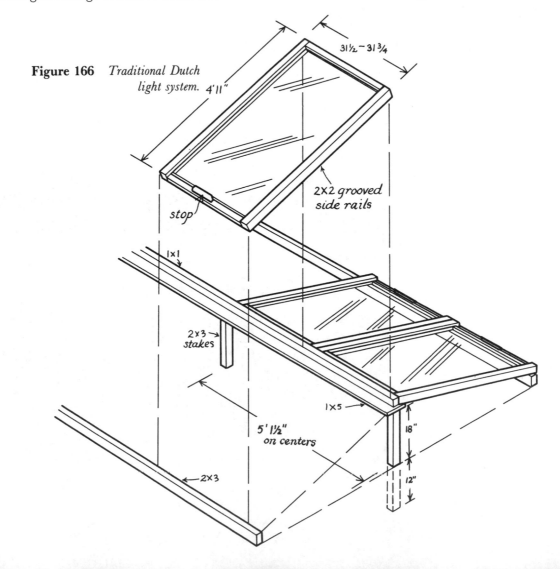

**Figure 166**  *Traditional Dutch light system.*

4'11"

31½ – 31¾

2x2 grooved side rails

stop

1x1

2x3 stakes

1x5

5'1½" on centers

18"

2x3

12"

Because the frames were portable, the lights were often moved from bed to bed as the growing season progressed. They were also frequently used to cover manure hotbeds during the colder seasons.

The use of lights faded from the scene during the middle of the twentieth century, but recent concerns about the need for reviving local agriculture in the Northeast have spurred the Coolidge Center for the Advancement of Agriculture in Topsfield, Massachusetts, to revive the Dutch Light system. Director Eliot Coleman has successfully obtained a grant from the Federal Government to build a collection of lights which will be used in both the traditional fashion and as components for small temporary greenhouses. The project will strive to demonstrate that these methods can be used economically by farmers to produce out-of-season and extra-early crops of a number of vegetables.

## The Cold Frame

Today's cold frame is probably one of the most useful devices in the garden (see Figure 168). It is really just a contemporary version of the traditional lights, but its role has been expanded to include:

Raising early crops of cold hardy greens and root crops.

Hardening off seedlings started in greenhouses or indoors.

Starting heat-loving crops like tomatoes, peppers, and melons in pots or flats.

Providing additional heat to summer crops of cucumbers and melons.

Protecting early fall crops of frost-susceptible plants.

Protecting late fall crops of cold hardy greens and root crops.

Protecting half-hardy perennials and biennials from severe winter cold.

A cold frame, minus its sash covering, can be used to support shading material over midsummer crops like lettuce that prefer cooler temperatures.

There are many ways to build a cold frame, and its design is limited only by the ingenuity of the builder. Its basic components are:

1. *A wooden or masonry base.* Like the bases for the traditional European lights, the frame should be de-

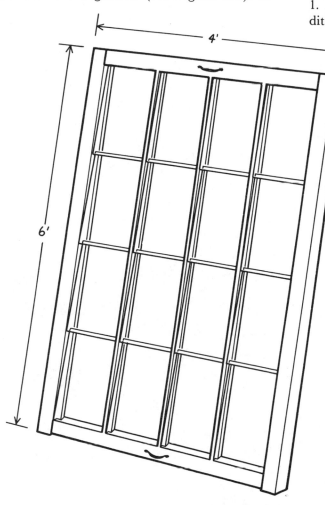

**Figure 167** *Traditional English lights: The frames are 6 feet by 4 feet in size, and the lights themselves are glazed glass with panes from 8 inches by 10 inches in size up to 12 inches by 18 inches.*

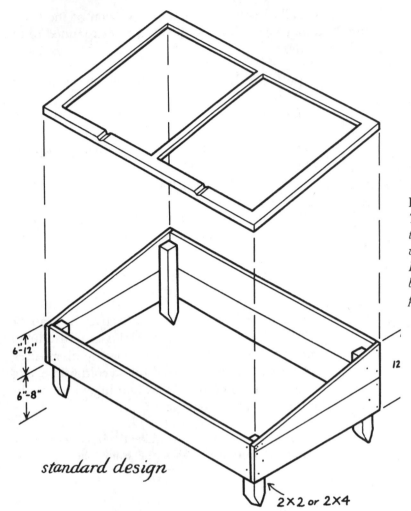

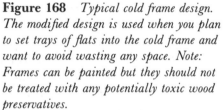

**Figure 168** *Typical cold frame design. The modified design is used when you plan to set trays of flats into the cold frame and want to avoid wasting any space. Note: Frames can be painted but they should not be treated with any potentially toxic wood preservatives.*

6"-12"

6"-8"

12

standard design

2×2 or 2×4

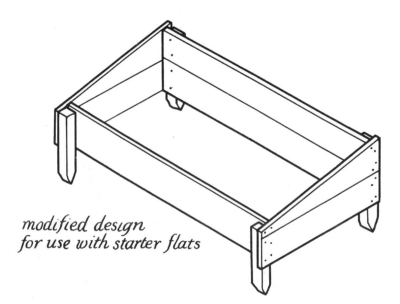

modified design
for use with starter flats

signed to slope to the south, but unlike traditional designs, the angle can be as much as 60° from horizontal. The farther north you live, the steeper the angle must be to obtain the maximum amount of spring and fall sunlight (see Figure 169). A general rule of thumb is that the optimum angle is equal to the geographic latitude at which you live. For us in New Hampshire this means that the optimum angle would be about 45°. If you live in central Ohio it would be 40°. The farther south you live, the lower the angle can be. This is not a hard rule, however, and you can still have a successful cold frame with an angle as low as 15° to 20°. A steeper angle will provide more sun but limit the amount of growing space. The lower angle will provide the maximum growing space but not capture the sun as well during the days of late fall.

Size is a matter of individual preference. The most convenient width ranges from 3 to 4 feet. Wider than this will result in your having difficulty reaching plants at the back of the frame. The length should be determined by how heavy a window you can lift. A

length of 4 to 6 feet is most common; longer frames result in unwieldy covers. If you are using old storm windows for your covers, you should preplan your frames to match the window sizes.

If you are building a permanent cold frame, you can use concrete blocks or bricks for the base. Dig a trench at least 1 foot deep (2 feet in very cold climates) to prevent frost from heaving up your frame, then lay in your blocks. You can simply set the blocks in place or use mortar if you want a more permanent frame. A wooden frame should be made either of rot-resistant wood (cypress, cedar, locust) or other wood treated with a preservative. Do not use creosote or pentachlorophenol, as these substances are toxic to plants and many animals.

A permanent wood frame should be set 8 to 10 inches into the ground. We recommend using full 1-inch thick lumber so that the corners can be connected with 3-inch lag bolts. If you use lighter wood, you will have to add two-by-two corner supports inside the frame. If you want to be able to move your frame from place to place, you need not make it as

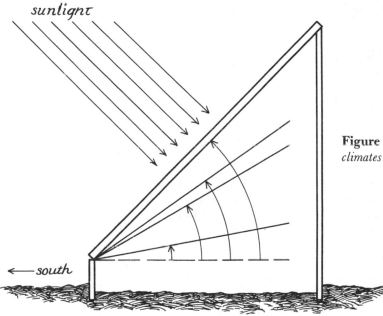

**Figure 169** *Cold frame angles for northern climates (regions north of 40° latitude).*

*up to 10° – good for use in spring, summer, early fall*
*about 30° – best for early spring and fall use*
*not less than 35° – good for year round use\**
*not less than 45° – best for late fall through early spring\**

*\* in most cases you will have to insulate frames which are to be used in late fall and winter*

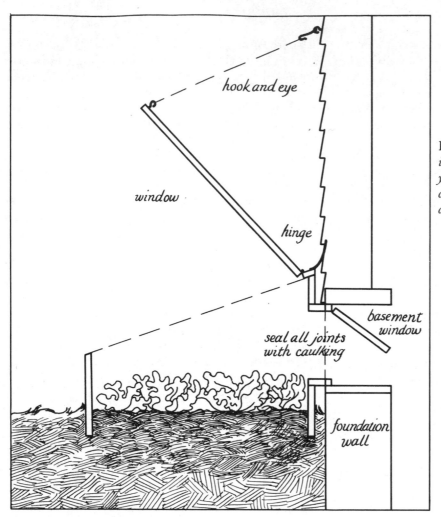

hook and eye

window

hinge

seal all joints
with caulking

basement
window

foundation
wall

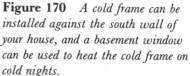

**Figure 170** *A cold frame can be installed against the south wall of your house, and a basement window can be used to heat the cold frame on cold nights.*

deep. The movable frame should be about 6 to 8 inches high on the south side, however.

Siting your frame will also depend upon whether or not it is to be permanent. A permanent frame can be installed against the south wall of a building and gain from the warmth of reflected sunlight and the heat of the foundation. Some gardeners even place their frames in front of a basement window to give the plants a bit of warm air on cold nights (see Figure 170). Movable cold frames must be oriented to face south, which means that if you are using them in your summer garden, your beds should run east to west. This runs counter to the best bed orientation, which is north to south, but we have solved the problem in our garden by giving both orientations equal rights—half of our beds run one way and half the other (see Figures 171–173).

2. *Insulation.* This is optional for the cold frame, though recommended if you want to get the maximum use over the entire year. Options range from piling hay bales up against the sides, berming earth up around the sides, and piling hot manure all around, to fully excavating down to the frost line and attaching boards of polystyrene insulation. We tend to favor the quick and dirty methods of piling material around the frame, saving our money for boards of insulation around the fancier Solar Pods and solar frame.

It is also necessary to insulate the cover of the cold frame on occasion. Most single-glazed frames will protect against frost when outdoor temperatures are above about 25 ° F. Double-glazed covers can protect down to about 15 ° F. On windy nights neither type can protect much below an outdoor temperature of 30 ° F unless your covers are well fitted and sealed. If you want to keep the frost out when the weather gets worse than this, you will have to cover the top with insulation at night. This can be done somewhat effectively with old blankets or pieces of plywood. Some gardeners have simply thrown loose hay over the top. If you are really determined to save your plants until Christmas, you can cut pieces of poly-

124

PHOTO BY PAUL DOSCHER.

**Figure 171** *A typical cold frame being used to harden-off spring seedlings.*

PHOTO BY TIMOTHY FISHER.

**Figure 172** *This small greenhouse is used as a walk-in cold frame.*

PHOTO BY TIMOTHY FISHER.

**Figure 173** *Portable A-frame cold frames being used in the garden of Adam and Bonnie Tomash in Maine to protect peppers and eggplant in the summer.*

styrene insulation to the right size and lay them on top of the frame. Be sure to hold them down with bricks, boards, or some heavy object so that they don't blow away.

3. *The window.* Any old storm window will do the job, but some are better than others. If you can, choose one with a minimum number of mullions and panes. The more panes, the more sunlight is blocked by the mullions. On the other hand, if you anticipate that kids, dogs, and acts of nature might find your window an attractive target, it is certainly less expensive to replace small panes than larger ones. Be sure to use only windows that are not rotten around the edges, as the warm environment of the cold frame will only accelerate the decay process. A coat of white paint will help slow the process of rotting and should be applied to all wooden parts. Be sure, however, to use paint that is lead-free.

If you cannot find the old window you want a simple cold frame cover can be made using 1-by-3-inch boards. This window frame can be glazed with polyethylene plastic or rigid fiberglass. Both of these materials are light enough for you to use a double layer to improve the heat efficiency of your cold frame.

Early cold frames were designed without hinges to hold the sash on top. This was done so that the frames could always be ventilated on the leeside (downwind) to avoid letting cold drafts into the growing area and to prevent wind gusts from picking up the sash and smashing them. Unfortunately, this also makes the cover somewhat unwieldy, and we recommend using hinges, even though they restrict your options in providing ventilation.

The window should be hinged at the back side. It is also advisable to provide a way to attach the window to a building or post when it is wide open. An open cold frame cover is easily blown over and shattered unless firmly anchored.

### Solar Pods

Another design by Leandre Poisson, the Solar Pod, is a modern, very efficient version of the cold frame. The nature of the weather in New England is such that uninsulated cold frames cannot provide as long a growing season as Poisson wants. His goal was to provide a growing season, in the garden, permitting cold hardy crops to be grown for fresh consumption during ten months of the year. He succeeded in doing this by developing a double-glazed, fully insulated device he named the Pod (see Figures 174–176).

The Pod can do all the cold frame can, and more. Because it is double glazed it can protect fall crops at outdoor temperatures down to around 10° F. The insulation used to surround the base of the Pod helps keep soil warm and promotes continued growth of late season crops right up until harvest. In the spring the soil in the Pod can be worked very early, and is warm enough to plant in long before outdoor garden soil.

**Figure 174** *A Solar Pod in early spring.*

PHOTO BY PAUL DOSCHER.

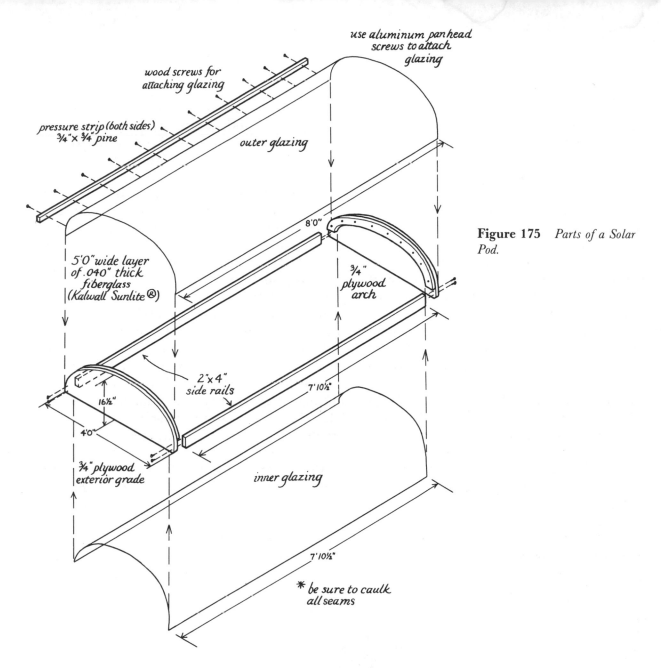

use aluminum pan head
screws to attach
glazing

wood screws for
attaching glazing

pressure strip (both sides)
¾" × ¾" pine

outer glazing

8'0"

**Figure 175**  *Parts of a Solar Pod.*

5'0" wide layer
of .040" thick
fiberglass
(Kalwall Sunlite®)

¾"
plywood
arch

2"× 4"
side rails

7'10½"

16½"

4'0"

¾" plywood
exterior grade

inner glazing

7'10½"

\* be sure to caulk
all seams

**Figure 176**  *Insulation for Solar Pods.*

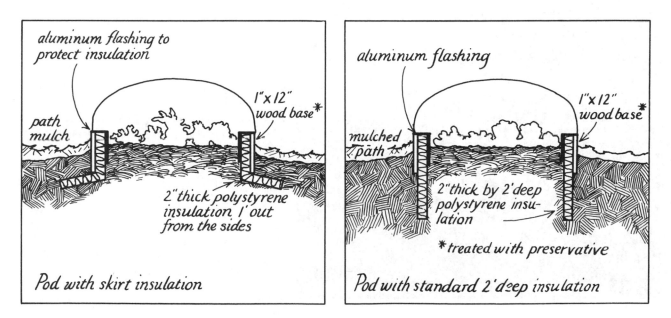

aluminum flashing to
protect insulation

path
mulch

1"× 12"
wood base \*

2" thick polystyrene
insulation 1' out
from the sides

Pod with skirt insulation

aluminum flashing

mulched
path

1"× 12"
wood base \*

2" thick by 2' deep
polystyrene insu-
lation

\* treated with preservative

Pod with standard 2' deep insulation

Pods are constructed of plywood, two-by-fours, and clear rigid fiberglass. The ¾-inch plywood (exterior grade) is used for the end pieces of each Pod, and two layers of fiberglass provide the glazing. The curved profile of the Pod allows plants considerable "head room" while also capturing sunlight as the sun moves across the sky. Unlike the cold frame, the Pod is always oriented in a north/south direction.

The Pod is designed to cover a 4-by-8-foot permanent bed. The reason for this somewhat large size is because the materials used to construct the Pod are costly, and the 4-by-8-foot size conserves materials and creates little waste. This makes for a somewhat heavy device, requiring two people to lift it. Once in place, however, it can be tipped up easily by one person.

The unwieldy size of the Pod could be reduced in length if desired, to 4, 5 or 6 feet. This would make it possible for one person to lift the cover, but would not really save any work in construction, although it would save in material costs.

The base for the Pod is a permanent, intensive bed, framed in wood (2-by-12-inch rough cut boards), which go down about 4 to 6 inches into the ground. A number of these bases can be built in a row to form a long bed.

The base is insulated from the top of the boards down to a depth of 18 to 24 inches. Insulation can be installed either on the inside or outside of the frame, but in both cases must be protected from damage by a covering of sheet metal, wood, or plastic. Polystyrene board insulation is used because of its low cost and relative durability. Two-inch-thick insulation is recommended by Poisson for the New England climate. In milder climates 1-inch insulation will probably be adequate, and if you live in an area where the temperature rarely drops below 20° F, you could probably get away without using any.

If getting the insulation down 18 to 24 inches into the ground is a problem (as it is in our garden, which has a high water table much of the year), you can use the "skirt system." This involves using insulation to the same depth as the bottom of the boards that form the base (1 foot), then running a one-foot horizontal skirt around the entire base. This will prevent frost from getting down into the ground around the Pod, thus keeping the Pod soil warm (see Figure 176).

Also used in the Solar Pod is a 55-gallon drum filled with water for heat storage (see Figure 177). The drum is painted black and installed at the north end of the base. Its purpose is to absorb solar heat during the day, hold it until night, and release it to keep the Pod environment warm. An added advantage of the drum is that the solar energy absorbed by it is enough to help hold down

**Figure 177** *Tests by Steve Tracy at the Community Organic Gardening project in Ashland, Massachusetts indicate that the use of drums filled with water as thermal mass can improve the performance of Solar Pods. These drums act to keep daytime temperatures a few degrees lower and nighttime temperatures as much as 10° warmer than in Pods without drums.*

PHOTO BY PAUL DOSCHER.

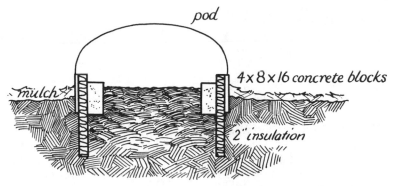

**Figure 178** *Concrete blocks can be used to provide a small amount of thermal mass without reducing the planting area substantially.*

the daytime temperatures in the Pod, reducing the need for ventilation. The most significant problem with using this method of thermal storage is the space it occupies. It reduces the amount of growing space in the Pod by about 5 square feet.

Another way to add some thermal mass to Pods or any cold frame is to place a number of water-filled, plastic jugs inside. This will not allow as much heat storage as a drum, but the jugs can be placed in locations where they will not take up as much space. Jugs can also be easily removed later in the spring to allow more growing space for summer crops.

We have also used concrete blocks for thermal storage of heat (see Figure 178). A number of 4-inch-wide blocks are set into the Pod base around the perimeter. The advantage of this is that the blocks do not really take up any planting space, since most plants must be spaced at least 4 inches from the sides of the base anyway. The blocks also provide a convenient place to step when working the soil or reaching in to harvest crops. Unfortunately, concrete captures and holds only a quarter of the heat per cubic foot that water does, and the heat storage value of our block perimeter is probably very limited.

You could actually build the permanent bed bases themselves from concrete or concrete blocks and "kill two birds with one stone." The base would then become both support for the Pod and provide some heat storage. As with the standard method used by Leandre Poisson, the base must be insulated, only with concrete the insulation must be placed on the outside.

If the snow is brushed off after every winter storm, the Solar Pod is capable of producing fresh crops until mid-December, and begins producing

as early as March in the spring. The normal frost-free growing season in southern New Hampshire extends only from mid-May to mid-September, so the Solar Pod adds as much as six months to the growing season. In milder climates it would probably be reasonable to expect the Pod to provide a year-round salad and root crop season.

The Solar Pod holds potential for market gardening applications as well. In Ashland, Massachusetts, the Community Organic Gardening Project, under the direction of Steve Tracy, has constructed forty-eight Solar Pods and is using them to spur renewed interest in community food self-reliance (see Figures 179–181). Eventually Tracy hopes to have a quarter of an acre under Pods. The initial funding for the project came from a grant by the U.S. Department of Energy.

The biggest drawback to the Solar Pod is cost. Tracy has calculated that it cost the Community Organic Gardening Project just over $62 (at 1979 prices) to buy the materials for one Pod and $64 for the materials to build the insulated base. This does not include any costs for labor or tools needed to construct the Pods. Although this may seem like a high cost, Tracy has gone on to calculate that it pays a healthy return in fresh produce. He estimates that the value of the produce from the Pods is such that the initial investment is recovered in about two years. If well maintained, the Solar Pods should last for over ten years, resulting in a significant long-term benefit from the initital $126 (per 4-by-8-foot Pod) investment.

Kits for the Solar Pod, including the plywood ends, hardware, and glazing material are sold by Solar Survival, and price information can be obtained by writing to Solar Survival, Box 275, Harrisville, New Hampshire 03450.

---

The term "Solar Pod" is a trademark of Solar Survival, Box 275, Harrisville, New Hampshire 03450.

**Figure 179**   *The Solar Pods at the Ashland Community Garden Project in Massachusetts.*

**Figure 180**   *Lettuce and Pak Choi in a Solar Pod at the Ashland Community Garden Project in Massachusetts.*

**Figure 181**   *Chinese cabbage in the early spring in Solar Pods at the Ashland Community Garden Project in Massachusetts.*

130

## SOLAR HOT FRAMES

The next step beyond lights, cold frames, and Solar Pods is a device efficient enough at collecting and storing solar heat to produce crops year-round in northern climates. When most people think of year-round growing, they think of greenhouses, and the solar hot frame is essentially a minigreenhouse—a hybrid between the cold frame and the modern solar greenhouse.

There are a number of designs for solar hot frames, but most look like a beefed-up version of a cold frame. The basic components are:

1. A fully insulated base that provides a fairly steep (30° to 60°) sloped south-facing exposure. The steep slope allows for maximum solar energy capture during the short, cold days of winter. The insulation is usually rigid polystyrene boards (a minimum of R-11 or 3 inches thick is recommended), which go far enough into the ground to prevent any frost from penetrating into the frame. The insulation is placed on the outside of the frame and must be covered by earth, wood, or metal. Polystyrene is gradually deteriorated by the ultraviolet rays of the sun, and any insulation left exposed will have to be replaced after only a few years.

2. All solar hot frames are double glazed to minimize heat loss. The most common material used is translucent fiberglass, because it is less fragile and can be used in larger sheets than glass. Polyethylene plastic can also be used.

3. The most effective frames incorporate an insulating shutter that covers the glazing at night, further reducing heat loss.

4. Thermal mass in the form of masonry, rocks, or tanks of water is used to store solar heat for nighttime use. Some frames incorporate the use of fermenting manure to provide additional warmth.

The Organic Gardening and Farming Research Center in Emmaus, Pennsylvania, has developed a device they call the Solar Grow Frame (see Figure 182). It is a fully insulated device, double glazed with fiberglass, and has a slope of about 60° on the south side (see Figure 183). It does not incorporate any permanent thermal storage, but the staff at the Research Center reports being able to grow many crops right through the Pennsylvania winter. They indicate they can keep soil temperatures in the 40's inside the Solar Grow Frame, which appears adequate for promoting continued growth in crops like Chinese cabbage.

The device we have used is called the Solar Frame and was developed by Leandre Poisson (see Figure 184). It incorporates all the advantages of the Rodale Grow Frame but adds three 30-gallon tanks of water for thermal storage, and an integrated, insulated shutter. The shutter is constructed of fiberglass, two-by-fours, and plywood. A reservoir of small polystyrene beads at the top of the shutter is kept closed during the day, using a valve. Once the sun goes down, the valve is opened, and the thousands of beads flow downward into the cavity formed by the two-by-fours

**Figure 183**  *Parts of a Solar Grow Frame.*

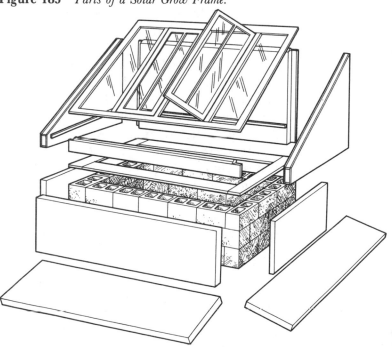

**Figure 182**  *The Solar Grow Frame at the Rodale Organic Gardening and Farming Research Center in Pennsylvania. Detailed construction plans can be purchased from the Rodale Press.*

PHOTO BY TIMOTHY FISHER.

PHOTO BY PAUL DOSCHER.

**Figure 184** *The Solar Frame designed by Leandre Poisson and developed by Paul Doscher. The round reservoir at the top holds styrofoam beads which are allowed to flow downward between the layers of glazing at night.*

**Figure 185** *Parts of a Solar Frame. Detailed construction plans are available from Solar Survival in Harrisville, New Hampshire.*

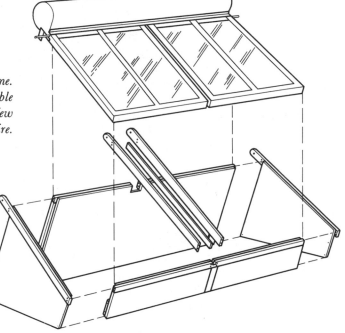

and the glazing. In tests at our New Hampshire location the air in the frame never dropped below 32° F all winter. (Nighttime temperatures can drop to −25° F in our location.) In the morning the shutter is lifted up on its hinges, and the beads flow back into the reservoir. The valve is then closed and the cover returned to the closed position, allowing sunlight to enter the frame for the day (see Figure 185).

The most significant problem with the Solar Frame is the tendency of the tiny beads to stick to the condensation on the fiberglass glazing when the shutter is lifted in the morning. This reduces the amount of sun entering the frame and can have a detrimental effect on plant growth. Additionally, the necessity to open the shutter cover each morning allows a burst of cold air into the frame. We have not noticed that this does any significant damage to the plants, but suspect that it is harmful just the same. Despite the disadvantages our Solar Frame has produced good crops of lettuce, Swiss chard, broccoli, Chinese cabbage, and radishes through three winters.

To cope with the problem of the insulating beads reducing the light-gathering ability of the Solar Frame, we have developed a design that separates the glazing from the shutter (see Figure 186). A lightweight double-glazed cover is constructed, and a folding shutter is used to cover the glazing at night. This eliminates both the use of loose beads (which become a giant nuisance if they escape from the shutter of the Solar Frame) and the need to expose the plants to cold morning air when opening the shutter.

The initial cost of a solar hot frame may vary considerably. Our Solar Frame materials cost about $250, but we suspect that with the rapid inflation of material costs, you should plan on spending at least $300 to build a solar hot frame. Of course, if you are willing to accept less efficiency and reduced crop production during the coldest months of January, February, and early March, you can build lower-cost hot frames using polyethylene and recycled materials.

Plans for the Poisson Solar Frame are available by writing to Solar Survival, Box 275, Harrisville, New Hampshire 03450. Information on plans for the Rodale Grow Frame and other hot frame designs is available by writing to the Organic Gardening and Farming Research Center, Emmaus, Pennsylvania 18049.

If you have the inclination, you can design and build your own version of the solar hot frame. This is a relatively new field, and we are sure that many new designs for shutters, frames, and other related devices are yet to appear as more and more people experiment in solar intensive gardening.

## THE SOLAR GREENHOUSE

Solar intensive gardeners will undoubtedly be interested in the extension of intensive garden techniques into the greenhouse. Although greenhouses are not truly solar intensive gardening devices, they do have great value to the gardener. The modern solar greenhouse, which heats itself and produces crops at the same time, is of particular interest. These structures are especially useful for starting flats of transplants for the garden, and have the ability to grow many crops through the entire winter (see Figures 187–189).

The principle behind the solar greenhouse is simple: The sun in allowed to shine in during the day, warming the air and a substantial quantity of thermal mass material. At night the greenhouse is well insulated to prevent heat from escaping to the outdoors, and the heat in the thermal mass contributes to keeping the air warm enough to allow continued plant growth.

Solar greenhouses face to the south and have little or no glass on the east and west walls. The pitch of the roof is usually matched to the latitude of the site, although some greenhouses have roofs at angles of up to 70°. In all but the mildest climates solar greenhouses are double glazed to re-

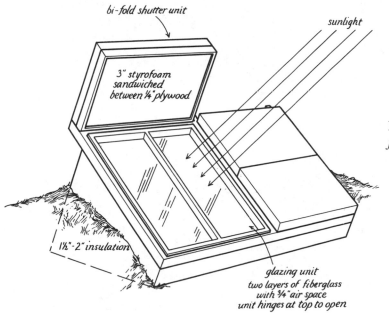

**Figure 186** *A Solar Frame design with folding shutter.*

bi-fold shutter unit

sunlight

3" styrofoam sandwiched between ¼" plywood

1½"-2" insulation

glazing unit
two layers of fiberglass
with ¼" air space
unit hinges at top to open

**Figures 187, 188, 189** *Solar greenhouse styles.*

PHOTO BY PAUL DOSCHER.

PHOTO BY PAUL DOSCHER.

PHOTO BY PAUL DOSCHER.

duce heat loss. The most efficient solar greenhouses also incorporate thermal shutters to cover the glazing at night, further reducing heat loss.

Any solar greenhouse will gain more heat during a sunny day than it can use. This will lead to overheating unless the heat can be somehow removed. Most often this is done by venting the greenhouse into an adjacent room in the building that the greenhouse is attached to. In this way the greenhouse also helps cut the heating costs of the adjacent home or office. In fact, most solar greenhouses are designed primarily for this heating function and only secondarily for producing plant crops.

From a strictly economic point of view, the solar greenhouse is probably not a wise investment if your only concern is growing edible plants for a number of reasons:

1. Greenhouses are considerably more expensive to build than any other solar intensive device. A simple 200-square-foot greenhouse with 100 square feet of growing space will cost a minimum of $1,500 to build, even though you do most of the construction yourself. The cost can go as high as $10,000 if you really get fancy.

2. Greenhouses require much more maintenance than other devices and demand that the owner become well versed in the skills of greenhouse horticulture.

3. Most solar greenhouses are designed primarily as heating devices, not plant environments. The closed east and west walls reduce the amount of light that can reach plants; this can result in lower-than-desired production levels. The need to capture solar heat for nighttime use requires that a substantial amount of the space in a solar greenhouse be occupied by thermal mass: drums, tubs of water, concrete, brick, or other means. This reduces the amount of space for plantings.

Does this mean that solar greenhouses are a waste of money? Not by any means. The greatest economic benefit of a solar greenhouse is likely to come in the heat it supplies to your home. With oil prices rising all the time, the contribution of solar heat can reduce the heating bills of a small, insulated home by as much as 50 percent. There are other benefits as well. Having a bright, warm, sunny space for reading, eating, or resting can be an invaluable asset in the dead of winter. Seeing green plants all around can provide significant psychological benefits to sufferers of cabin fever, and might even save you the cost of taking a winter vacation to warmer climes!

Of course there is the value, however meager in economic terms, of eating fresh-grown greens and vegetables during a season that finds everyone else eating canned goods, frozen produce, or seven-day-old vegetable imports from California.

But in the final analysis a solar greenhouse is really a step beyond solar intensive gardening. The solar intensive gardener may well choose to build a greenhouse, but if your only objective is food production, solar intensive devices are more cost effective.

## ACCESSORIES AND OTHER USEFUL DEVICES

Any solar intensive device is really a solar oven in disguise. Leave it closed on a warm day and you'll discover why baked lettuce is not on anyone's list of gourmet delights. This need to provide regular ventilation can be met by manual means, or, if your solar device covers are not too heavy, by automatic venting devices like those common in commercial greenhouses. The vent opener is a thermostatically controlled lifting device which can automatically open a cold frame or hot frame window weighing up to 26 pounds (see Figure 190). It requires no source of power because it contains an expanding cylinder powered by the heat of the sun. As the cylinder expands, the arm

**Figure 190** *This solar-operated automatic venting device can help take some of the risk out of solar intensive gardening.*

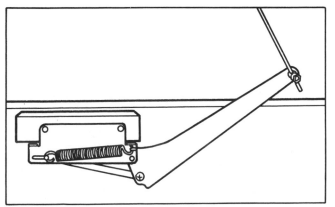

of the device opens. This ingenious device can be obtained in many garden stores and through some seed catalogs. It comes in models that lift up to 12 pounds and spring-assisted versions that lift as much as 26 pounds. Costs range from around $26 to $30.

Also available through many garden stores are miniature, automatically vented cold frames (see Figure 191). They are small enclosures made of acrylic plastic and wood and have an automatic opener that vents the device at temperatures of about 70–80° F. The size of these devices tends to be small (about 3 by 4 feet is the maximum), but this is a good piece of equipment for hardening off seedlings or extending the season for small foliage crops. They cost in the range of $60 to $70.

There are other devices similar to the ones mentioned above, and we have no doubt that most of them work well and live up to the claims of their manufacturers. The major problem with most of them, however, is cost. You can build your own cold frame out of scrap wood and windows or polyethylene, and then buy an automatic opener for probably less than half the price of a commercially available device. If you plan on having a number of cold frames, hot frames, or other devices, this economic consideration will be very important.

Another important piece of equipment to have in your solar intensive garden is a minimum-maximum thermometer (see Figure 192). There are a variety of models on the market, ranging in price from a few dollars up to over $20. If you want to have a number of them placed in various locations around the garden, the less expensive models will be your best choice. The problem with some of these cheaper thermometers is accuracy. We have noticed that there can be a significant variation between individual thermometers of the same brand and model. To minimize this problem it is wise to bring all your thermometers indoors, and set them for a few hours next to a thermometer you know to be accurate. Then calibrate the thermometers so that they all read the same. This can usually be accomplished by turning a small screw on the back side. If you have mercury thermometers, there is little you can do to correct for inaccuracy unless the scale is on an adjustable plate.

**Figure 191** *Small, automatic, miniature cold frames can be very helpful for hardening-off transplants.*

For the most accurate records min-max thermometers must be reset every day. What we have done is reset the thermometers in the morning, recording the minimum and maximum temperatures of the previous twenty-four hours on a calendar. This gives us an accurate record of how our devices are performing and also lets us know how warm our crops were getting while we were away

**Figure 192** *A minimum-maximum thermometer.*

during the day. This helps in making decisions on changes in ventilation or on the use of more or less insulation in the next device we build.

A soil thermometer is essential for determining when to plant (see Figures 136 and 193). There are a few inexpensive models to choose from, and, based upon our experience, all are satisfactory. Choose one with a temperature-sensing probe that is at least 6 inches long so that you can get accurate readings for early spring planting. It is not necessary to leave your soil thermometers in the ground all the time. They respond quickly to changes in temperature, and can be inserted to any depth at any time for a quick temperature reading.

For the summer intensive garden there are a number of homemade devices that can act to provide thermal assistance without actually covering

**Figure 193** *A soil thermometer.*

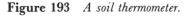

Figure 194  *Ray Nelson uses old tires and plastic cloches to speed the growth of his melons in Maine.*

unsightly garden, but there is little doubt that the black rubber can absorb a lot of solar heat. If the tire is partly buried in the ground around a plant, much of this warmth will be conducted into the soil. Another advantage some gardeners claim for the tires is that they catch rainwater and hold it for days when the plants require a little moisture. On the day the water is needed you use a strong stick to push down on the inner rim of the tire, letting the water seep into the soil. This may be fine for periods when the need for water is minimal, but we doubt that any tire could contain enough water, long enough, to make much of a difference during a real dry spell.

Black plastic mulch is also a help in providing warmer conditions for heat-loving crops. In most cases we prefer to use organic mulches, because

Figure 195  *Gretchen Poisson uses old tires and solar cones to induce rapid growth in these cantaloupes in New Hampshire.*

plants. We have come across gardeners who have filled jugs with water, painted them black, then buried them halfway into the soil next to a heat-loving tomato plant. This will help to warm the soil a little and keep it slightly warmer at night.

Another idea is to ring a bed of heat-loving plants with concrete blocks, bricks or rocks. The rocks and concrete absorb heat all day long and slowly release it at night, providing a warming effect. In cooler climates this could be of great benefit because it is nighttime temperatures in the low 50's that really slow down the development of tomatoes, peppers, eggplant, and melons (see Figures 194 and 195). The slight warming provided by the rocks and concrete may be just enough to make a difference between crop success or failure for some gardeners.

Along the same line is the use of old tires. This idea creates what some people consider to be an

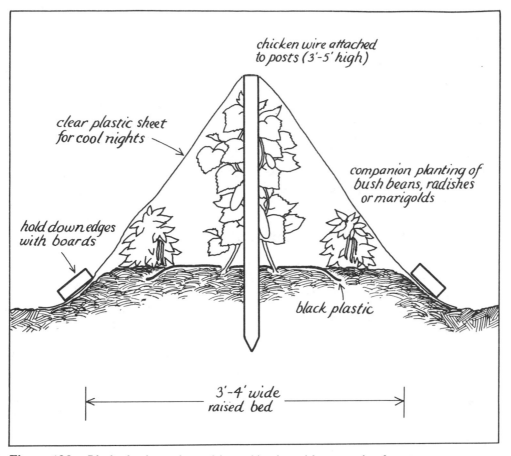

**Figure 196** *Black plastic can be used in combination with a cucumber fence to provide a number of benefits.*

they can later be turned into the soil, but for cucumbers and melons we have found black plastic to be superior (see Figure 196). In our New Hampshire garden we get very early frosts, and even during the summer months often experience nighttime temperatures in the high 40's. This made it almost impossible to produce much of a cucumber or melon crop in the open garden until we started using black mulch. The extra heat apparently made the difference, and we now have successful and bountiful crops of melons and cucumbers. Part of the key to our success may have been that we did not allow the plants to sprawl all over the plastic, thus shading it from the sun's rays. Instead, we grew the plants up a chicken wire fence, which was run right down the middle of the bed after the seedlings and mulch were in place. The fence can also be used as a support for a polyethylene cover to protect the cukes from cold night air or early frosts.

This brings us to the common need for intensive gardeners to conserve space. There are many ways to provide trellises, poles, and fences for plants like melons, peas, cucumbers, beans, and such to grow on. Most of us are familiar with the traditional bean poles and pea fences, but intensive gardeners should also consider using their solar intensive devices for this purpose. If you are going to build a tunnel cloche for the spring, why not make the framework strong enough to keep in the garden all summer long? Once you have removed your early crops, you can plant climbing plants that will use the supports. Adding strings or wires between the supports will provide you some additional climbing room. If the framework is tall enough, it can even be used as a support for polyethylene frost protection in the fall. We have done this with all sorts of supporting devices, tomato cages, bean poles lashed together to form a tent, wire hoops, and wooden frames.

## CONCLUSION

There is no doubt that we have not covered all the possible solar intensive devices in this chapter. People are constantly coming up with new ideas and revised versions of old ideas. What we have tried to do is give you an overview of the types of devices you can use, and hope that you will experiment and develop your own ideas as well. The accompanying chart summarizes the properties of possible glazing materials for solar intensive devices.

Don't feel constrained by our recommendations. What works best in New England may not work best in Oregon or Wisconsin. The point is not that you should try hard to duplicate the work of the nineteenth-century French intensive gardeners or our work. Your real objective should be to grow good food, produced inexpensively, as close to year-round as possible, using the energy of the sun.

## GLAZING MATERIALS FOR SOLAR INTENSIVE DEVICES

| Material | Trade Name and Manufacturer | Life | Flexible? | Cost | Notes |
|---|---|---|---|---|---|
| **Glass** | Numerous | Indefinite if not broken | No | Varies between $.40 to $1.00 per sq ft for single pane sheets | The best material for outer glazing of flat surfaced devices because it is completely resistant to degradation by ultraviolet light. Not recommended where breakage by snow loads or vandalism is a problem. |
| **Polyethylene Plastic Film** | Numerous | Three months in full sun, one year in northern areas | Very | Varies, but always relatively inexpensive | Easily torn or punctured. Highly degradable when exposed to UV light or high temperatures. Monsanto produces a "602" material which is UV stabilized and should last at least twice as long as conventional polyethylene. It is available through greenhouse suppliers. |
| **Fiberglass Reinforced Plastic (Polyester)** | Sunlite® Kalwall Corp. POB 237 Manchester, NH 03105 | Seven to twenty years depending upon grade | Yes | Between $.65 to $.96 per sq ft | Sunlite is a very good material for many devices. It is the material used for glazing the Solar Pod and Solar Frame by Leandre Poisson. Sunlite can be recoated with a liquid coating to extend its life. |
| | Filon® Vistron Corp. 2333 S. Van Ness Ave. Hawthorne, CA 90250 | Ten to twenty years | Yes | Similar to glass | Can be obtained with a coating which resists UV degradation. |

| Material | Trade Name and Manufacturer | Life | Flexible? | Cost | Notes |
|---|---|---|---|---|---|
| **Fiberglass Reinforced Plastic (cont.)** | Lascolite® Lasco Industries 8015 Dixon Drive Florence, KY 41042 | Ten to twenty years | Yes | Similar to glass | Can be obtained with coating to resist degradation |
| **Clear Polycarbonate** | Lexan® Rohm and Haas | NA | Slightly | Expensive, $2.50 to $3.50 per sq ft | Lexan is also produced as a double wall material known as Twinwall® It is not recommended for solar intensive devices because of its high cost. |
| | Poly-Glaz Sheffield Plastics POB 248 Salisbury Rd. Sheffield, MA 01257 | NA | Slightly | NA | Claimed to be light stable (nondegrading). |
| **Acrylic** | Plexiglas® Rohm and Haas | Ten to twenty years | Slightly | Between $1.00 to $2.50 depending on thickness | Scratches easily. Over 20% better insulator than glass. Acrylic has a tendency to undergo significant expansion and contraction with temperature changes. |
| **Fluorocarbon Film** | Teflon® DuPont Co. 10th and Market St. Wilmington, DE 19898 | Fifteen years | Very | NA | High temperature resistance. Good for inner glazings. Susceptible to tearing. |
| **Polyester Films** | Mylar® type W DuPont | Four years | Very | Very low | Use only weather treated types. Untreated mylar degrades very quickly. Good impact resistance. |
| **Polyvinyl Fluoride Film** | Tedlar® DuPont | Five to ten years | Very | Between $.15–$.20 per sq ft | Tedlar is used in many solar collectors as an inner glazing. Attracts dust. Good UV resistance; it is often used to coat other glazings to give them UV resistance. |

SOURCES:
*The Solar Age Products Directory* (*Solar Age* magazine, Church Hill, Harrisville, NH).
*The Solar Greenhouse Book,* edited by James McCullagh, Rodale Press.
*Getting the Most from Your Garden* by the editors of *Organic Gardening* magazine, Rodale Press.
Miscellaneous product information brochures.

## INDEX

Numbers in **boldface** refer to illustrations.

142